Opening To Life

*How you can heal the past,
live the Now & create the future
by opening to channel pure
Life Force energy.*

CW01497119

Paul D. Walsh-Roberts

LIFEOFLIGHT
M E D I A

Published by
LifeOfLight Media

www.lifeoflightmedia.com
info@lifeoflightmedia.com

ISBN: 0-908807-13-9

*Dedicated to all who are seeking
to participate and contribute meaningfully
in the birth of a new and
heightened reality.*

TABLE OF CONTENTS

THE JETTY

Everything—absolutely everything—was white as I walked onto the pristine wooden boards and looked out over the bay; varying shades of pale as though molded in milk or carved out of some peculiar substance, maybe white chocolate. And it was quiet... strangely quiet. I couldn't even hear the rippling water that lapped at the sturdy posts suspending the jetty in the warmth and stillness of the day.

White clouds drifted across a perfect white sky. At some distance to both left and right were white rocky outcrops covered in equally white trees.

White, white and more white. As far as the eye could see. Strange, but unspeakably beautiful.

Even he was dressed in white, perched on the end of the jetty with his feet dangling in the milky water. He obviously sensed me coming. As he turned to look into me, he appeared to be in his early twenties and totally at peace with my having arrived in his beautiful sanctuary. He beckoned me to sit beside him on the white wooden boards.

My feet touched the water with exactly the same ripples as his, almost as if they were the same feet in the same place. As they did, it was as though my entire body began filling from the feet upwards with a liquid calmness; a deep sense of well being.

"Hi," he said, without moving his lips one iota.

"Hi," I replied, trying not to stare at his motionless mouth. He smiled way past the horizon.

"What would you like to talk about?" The pause

was perfect, without expectation. "You've come here for a reason. Aren't you curious?"

But I just sat there, fascinated by the sensation of my body being filled with the liquid calm. We sat for a moment until I recalled his question.

"Who are you?" I asked.

"Michael."

"Oh," I responded loosely as my thoughts scanned my mind for Michaels I'd known. I hoped to recognize one of them in him but...

The conversation seemed endlessly inane and yet deeply profound, the time so lazy yet speeding by noticeably. An age, yet in no time at all...

Mandy's voice interjected at exactly the right time asking me to come back. From where? Oh yes, of course; this isn't real. I'm meant to come back to her group now and share this experience with the others.

I lifted my feet out of the water and stood peering down at Michael. My feet were not wet, and neither were the white boards beneath. I glanced into Michael's deep eyes, bottomless pools of peace and clarity.

"Well, I'll be off then. See you next time," I promised. He just smiled up at me and watched as I turned and walked towards the white mist.

If you've ever felt what it's like to know someone is standing behind you, almost touching you yet you can't see them, then you'll have some inkling of how I felt as I strode back up the jetty... supposedly away from Michael.

Even when I tried walking faster I felt his presence

still there, closer than ever. That had never happened before. I dared not look back as I felt my heart begin to pound. Immersing myself in the white fog, I assumed his presence would diminish. Instead, the feeling got even stronger while Mandy's voice called me back into the group, louder and clearer.

Becoming more aware of my body and sitting in the chair, I knew I was returning to my awareness of the room and the meditation group of which I'd become a regular member.

But Michael was still there! How could that be? Why hadn't he faded along with that illusion I'd experienced, the way it had all dissolved nicely away on every previous occasion? I could feel perspiration running down my face. Or was it tears?

As a last panicked resort to get a grip on my situation, I willed myself to open my eyes, knowing without any shadow of doubt that the feeling of having someone breathing down my neck would instantly disappear.

Eyes open...

Still there! Oh no! My heart began to pound even harder with dismay. I could feel the sensation of color draining out of my face, not to mention rivers of sweat. I felt panicked and delighted, intrigued and excited, hot and cold... all at once. My skin began itching and the perspiration was running down my entire body saturating my clothing. I could hear my breaths. In... out... in... out... I could feel my body buzzing excitedly as it expanded and contracted so determinedly.

Suddenly, the sensation of the presence surged. I couldn't help myself; I began laughing. I laughed and laughed and laughed. As I did, the feelings of concern caved in under sheer euphoria. I laughed uncontrollably for several minutes until tears were streaming down my face.

As the sensations subsided, I began feeling a deepening sense of loss. Anticlimax subdued my recollection as I described to the others my experience of the events that had transpired in my meditation. But their outward effects had certainly impacted the whole group. They were all openly astounded.

Back at home later that night, I tried unsuccessfully to sleep. I was certain I could feel every cell in my body, individually, humming. It was a sense of heightened awareness of myself; an aliveness that I'd never felt before. It was as though each cell was vibrating with some strange energy or force. Moreover, my bedroom felt as though it was crammed with people, though I couldn't see... which didn't help my sleeplessness.

I drifted off to sleep in the early hours of the morning, exhausted yet energized at the same time. I'd been lying there for several hours in some kind of time warp that made it seem like only minutes.

Over the next few weeks I experienced irregular spontaneous reoccurrences of my encounter with Michael. They were less intense and debilitating but significant nevertheless. I observed that my daily meditations were becoming even more clearly visual and 'real' and that I was experiencing deeper emotions in my day-to-day experiences.

My whole life was feeling more rich yet I felt

somehow as though I was watching it like a movie. I seemed to be merely a detached onlooker, even though it was also apparent that I could see and feel everything more vividly than ever before.

Most importantly, I realized that I'd pierced an inner barrier that normally existed between the reality that my embodied self considers real and another reality that my meditating self found equally real and vivid.

I hadn't merely stepped over that barrier in meditation, leaving my body on one side and allowing my purer mind to explore the other; it was more than that. Much more. I'd actually punctured the veil, permanently and irreversibly. I'd broken the barrier so that now the reality that lay beyond began leaking into this physical world of mine. As it did, it increasingly flooded my day-to-day life with the qualities and perspectives of higher consciousness; a much more vast perception and understanding of all things.

This tinted my experiences in so many ways, subtle at first but eventually fuelling changes in my life on a monumental scale. It enabled me to experience a deeper stillness and peace in the face of conflict and a profound awareness and appreciation of the magic that was truly occurring in myself and all life as I went about my day-to-day living; a magic and richness that I could not have even taken for granted earlier because I had simply never noticed it woven through my every moment.

Nothing seemed to escape the influence of this new energy which poured in that night and its presence remains an intrinsic part of my life to this day. It still brings transformation, realizations and healing into every facet of my life, all seemingly in accordance with some spontaneous-yet-planned, random-yet-intelligently-organized purpose.

In crossing some interdimensional boundary as I had, I—a regular person with mortgage, bank statements, lawns to mow on Saturday, credit card bills, car repayments, window envelopes in the mail, professional career in an office, and commitments and aspirations—had opened my life to a vast unimaginable journey of transformation and disruption, joy and wonder. Euphoria, along with a genuine sense of fulfillment.

A vital realization was that anyone can do it. I'm just as human and normal and average as anybody else, but by tapping into this force of energy from outside our normal universe of experience and acceptance, we avail ourselves all other universes of potential as well.

PREPARATION

Prior to the jetty event, my meditations with the group had basically taken the form of "I'll just go into my little quiet place and chat with my folk while the rest of the people in the group do their meditation." I had no real idea of what had been happening; that I'd actually been oblivious to the fact that I'd been preparing for this breakthrough.

Since my first few weeks in that meditation group, I'd been diligently meditating independently every morning. Even in those quiet times I was having discussions as well. More discussions about more things.

One morning, as I came out of my meditation and sat contemplating for a few moments before preparing to go into the office for work, a voice sounding as clear as crystal said "Take up your pen and paper." Startled, I opened my eyes and looked around to see if someone was standing nearby... Nobody.

Again, "Take up your pen and paper."

In my mind I said "But I've got to go to the office now. I've got a busy morning ahead."

Once again the voice, "Take up your pen and paper."

So I did. I rushed into another room, grabbed a pen and a note pad and sat down in the chair again, poised with pen in hand and mentally looking upwards expectantly as if to say "Okay, what now?"

Nothing. Absolutely nothing. I sat waiting for several minutes but... nothing. The office seemed a much more pressing matter, anyway.

Next morning, coming out of my meditation, again I heard the distinct voice "Take up your pen and paper." Immediately I rushed and returned armed with the writing materials.

Again, nothing. How frustrating, I thought. "Is someone there?" Nothing.

I got shrewd. The following morning I sat to meditate but this time with the pen and paper already at my side, lying on the wide arm of my usual big lounge chair. Coming out of meditation that day, there was the voice, "Take up your pen and paper."

Onto my lap I hastily grabbed them. Before I could say "There, gotcha!" my hand began scrawling rapidly across and down the page. I somehow knew that there was a transmission of some sense taking place, but no way did the writing convey anything I could read, let alone comprehend! It was looking as though a drunken spider with inked legs had been running aimlessly all over the page. Yet it kept flowing until coming to what felt like an intentional stop. An actual full stop happened then... stillness. Again that profound Nothing flooded the moment.

The letterhead size page was almost full—of scribble; illegible scribble. I knew something real and meaningful had transpired though; I felt a sense of achievement, of some result. But heaven only knew what it was about. I'd have to wait.

Waiting was not one of my strengths and I was almost impatient to get into my meditation the next day. The mere anticipation of the same sort of sensation and sense of meaning and achievement and purpose that had flooded me the previous morning now fuelled my focus and commitment. Sure enough, the meditation tapered off and I was becoming increasingly aware of being in the room and in my armchair again. Pen and paper were in my lap. Then— wham—the writing again.

This time it seemed a little more legible though more like some language I didn't recognize. On it went without pause until finishing suddenly with that intentional full stop again. I looked at it—one and a half pages this time; meaningless scrawls just like last time. But still that indefinable sense of achievement, of purpose... of meaning.

Each morning the writing became clearer and clearer and my eagerness and focus became almost an obsession. I used to run for fitness at that time and found that there comes a point during a run where you don't want to stop, ever. This felt a lot like that.

Several days had passed since that first call to "Take up your pen and paper." Now, I actually had 3 sheets of paper with reasonably legible writing. One sheet even included a simple drawing—a scene looking out over low flat land with a mountain range in the far distance and a tree nearby. It brought African savanna to mind, though I'd never set foot on that continent. The writing didn't seem very erudite or meaningful actually, taking more the form of an excerpt from some discussion where I hadn't heard the beginning or end portions. Never mind, it felt worth the daily discipline and I was now eager to see what it would all lead to.

As days, weeks and months passed, the writings

became fast, fluent and definitely meaningful. Each day's transmission seemed to cover a topic, perfectly encapsulated in almost exactly the same amount of writing. That efficiency I admired; it appealed to the Virgo in me. But it did astonish me, upon reflection... how did it manage to come within an almost exact quantity? Every time?

It was always so concise and exact and thorough within that consistent number of words. Yet the topics covered were so disparate: a soul's choices before birth; how rain and rivers are analogies for our emotional state; what anger really is; meditation methods and disciplines; the school of life; the body's infallible memory. Amazing; the same amount. Every time.

I must say, I'm a born skeptic. I believe that skepticism is very healthy. I've learned though, that there are two types of skepticism—the open minded and the closed minded varieties. The former is very healthy and encourages discernment in all things whilst also enabling one to learn and grow. The latter is very destructive to the individual, disabling learning and undermining the ability to expand consciousness and grow as a person.

Being a skeptic of the former variety, I'd actually spent a few months naively concocting my own version of a test for this writing phenomenon with which I'd now become irretrievably involved. It was a simple test that entailed me writing a topic at the head of a new sheet of paper before my meditation each morning so that I could see if it would be answered satisfactorily later. I didn't want to have to come out of my meditation and try to employ my rational mind to think of a topic whilst still in a semi meditative state. I wanted sensible everyday sorts of questions.

Without fail I received meaningful, satisfying, common sense—and, more often than not, astounding—answers. Again, constantly amazing. I even tried putting really crazy or sometimes innocuous questions to the test just to see what would happen, always getting a deeply significant and meaningful answer that felt like profound unshakeable Truth... all exactly the same quantity of writing!

On one occasion, getting a little complacent, even lazy, I put three completely unconnected, unrelated questions on three different sheets of paper so that for the next few days I wouldn't have to think up one each morning. Instead, I could just resurrect one of the sheets of paper, nominate the existing question written on it and enjoy the meditation and feedback. Lo and behold, on the first of the three mornings all three seemingly unrelated questions became answered in one transmission; three seemingly disparate subjects woven seamlessly together in a common sense way that showed they were in fact totally related and meant something profound... and all within that same quantity of text again!

What I ended up learning from my tests was that all things in life, regardless of whether they seem great or trivial, are in fact profoundly significant events in the stream of overall creation, as well as being opportunities for everyone involved to learn and grow if they bother to see the value in those moments. Furthermore, if we are willing to ask, be discerning and remain open to unexpected answers, there is an infinite wealth of wisdom waiting for us to tap into through the process of opening our own personal channels to the flow of higher consciousness that is perpetually available to us.

Relentlessly it came, day after day. The pages piled up and the questions became ever deeper and more poignant according to issues that were in my own life or that I was becoming aware of around me.

This process, I realized, was somehow enabling me to actually observe and perceive life very differently than I had before, with meaning and with value in every instant and every occurrence; with a distinct unshakeable understanding that, no matter what circumstances were prevailing or what issues seemed so important or unimportant, there was a deep, meaningful explanation and learning that was stored within it waiting to be released for the enlightenment of all concerned.

It was becoming so clear that the whole puzzle of life and the world, in all its disparate aspects, is entirely worthwhile and valuable and is, in fact, completely interconnected, not separate as I'd previously understood most things to be.

Seeing my life through these clearer eyes had a disconcerting effect eventually. I could now see clearly which parts of my own life had little real quality or meaning for me personally in terms of my learning and growth, and in some cases they were things I'd previously held dear to me.

As my awareness was shifting and transforming

and enriching, I found myself wanting to directly experience more of the vastness I could now see as being available in life.

The first really noticeable effect was a methodical editing of my attention and what I pointed it towards in life. I had a clearer idea of what felt truly important to me and I focused my attention on those things more and more while others faded into insignificance or out completely. There was nothing wrong with those fading aspects, it was just that I knew that they didn't hold in them a step on my path of growth other than the step of learning to let go of what is obsolete instead of trying to force it to work, or to work out. I had no right to try and make anyone or anything else change along with me.

Importantly, this editing was resetting my values and directions in life as well. Subtly at first, and really without deliberately doing it. Eventually I was evaluating and rebuilding my life consciously according to these unshakeable truths and principles that had developed through my encounters in meditation and my writings each morning. My own life became the testing ground, not indiscriminately but for the principles I learned that felt deeply true to me and that I felt were important to my own development as a person as well as for the highest good of one and all.

I couldn't turn back. Life was truly not what I'd thought it was. I didn't know exactly what it was but I knew it had a profound meaning and purpose beyond surface appearances. I also knew now that if I persisted with the writing and listening, the meaning that was locked inside each circumstance and experience would become apparent. Even the bad times were looking good!

It was at that time that I met Michael at the jetty and the encounter proceeded to flood my life with both euphoria and uncertainty. It was a sublime ambiguity that seemed to fuel some unspoken unconscious commitment I must have made to growing and learning. More to the point, a commitment that I was putting into action at every moment I felt able or sufficiently courageous. I'd like to say it was every moment but there was definitely a prolonged period spent adapting to this transformation, integrating it into what I'd previously thought was my life.

I'd been looking at life much more thoroughly than ever, putting to the test the very ideas and principles that came through in the writing and listening. It seemed that the jetty encounter had provided me the courage to do even more about sorting the wheat from the chaff in my life. I was moving on emotionally, professionally and even geographically. The urge to move on, in more ways than one, got stronger by the day.

My career in advertising, which I loved and for which I'd been fortunate enough to win international awards, now became rivaled by what had become my now rampant quest for wisdom, truth and insight into areas of existence that had never even occurred to me previously, and certainly to which I could find no real satisfying answers from any other source I'd come across. I was feeling quite detached, but not disconnected, from family and friends, my daily routines, even from my home and nation.

In my work I found that I was interacting with my clients on a much more personal basis, many of them discussing with me quite personal issues. It was as though people were unwittingly tapping into my inner guidance. I'd always considered such candor improper and unprofessional. I'd kept it all separate as long as I could but now it was transcending all barriers I'd ever built in my mind and life. Others were treating me much more as a confidant than a companion, another depth of involvement in people's lives that was growing despite my preconditioned beliefs that such things should not overlap in life for fear of compromising one or the other.

But I loved it. I loved helping real people with real day-to-day issues in their lives. It didn't drain me as I'd expected it would, it inspired and energized me the more I became aware of the depths of their issues and allowed my inner connectedness to bring the words and ideas through me and out into the world in these situations.

I found that as I spoke to individuals in casual conversation I'd have ideas and words springing to mind and from my lips that were new to me but absolutely pertinent to those people's personal issues, even healing and empowering, resolving conflicts, uncertainties and difficulties in their lives that had seemed otherwise insurmountable.

To me though, it all had the distinct flavor of

plagiarism about it (and that's something I'd seen enough of for several lifetimes, having spent a couple of decades in the creative side of the advertising business!). After all, I'd just chat with these people and the words would almost fall out my mouth accidentally. It was basically without thought at all; quite effortless, really, other than maintaining the discipline of keeping my rational mind out of the process so that it wouldn't interfere. I'd already witnessed the limiting effects of that rational mind infecting my life with its preconceptions, conditioning and biases accumulated over the previous few decades.

It was clear to me that the flow of words and ideas was pouring through me, not from me. I began to see the significance of learning to surrender to this flow of the same raw, formless unidentifiable energy that, back there a year ago at the Jetty, had overwhelmed me, tossing me way outside my comfort zone.

Though it'd felt unnerving, even distressing back then, it was now the source of such joy and fulfillment. I'd learned that something so disruptive can actually be an enormous gift if we allow it and trust in its clandestine purpose. Obviously, the energy hadn't changed at all; I had.

OPENING TO LIFE

Someone once said "Just because something is popular, that doesn't make it right; and just because it's right, it doesn't make it popular." That wisdom hit home to me then, and again frequently through the times since.

Wherever I traveled in the world and no matter who I was with or in what circumstance, I saw a valuable reason, a worthy purpose. I had clarity and understanding for even the most trivial as well as most profound things in life. Life definitely had value and purpose and was gratifyingly worthwhile, all qualities that had eluded me before.

I could see a real value to every moment in my life as well as in others', not to mention a burning desire growing inside me to share this with people since it offered a view of all things that proved to defuse conflicts, stresses and misunderstandings and to make sense where there'd appeared to be none prior. Even in situations where people appeared not to 'get it' I still found value. At the same time I was even able to fine tune what I'd learned and understood myself so that on another occasion it'd be even more clear and relevant.

Shedding the boundaries of my past had ejected me from the cocoon of safety and indifference into the vast wonderland of learning and growth that our world truly is. My travels took me largely through Asia, Europe, UK and USA, Australia and New Zealand. Until I found Hong Kong.

Hong Kong was like a coming of age for me; being given the key to my life and the higher spiritual realms. I remember vividly arriving in Hong Kong, a side stop on my way to Canada, and flying in over the coastline to Kai Tak Airport. The only thing apparent to me at the time was that I felt so strongly that I was coming home; which made absolutely no sense considering I'd never been to the Far East before at all. Nevertheless, I felt that strange impossible familiarity sweep over me and it stayed for years to come, just as I did there in that extraordinary and intoxicating city.

At that time my advertising career was still attractive to me in practical ways but I had a full fledged 'other life' bursting out. It was one of spiritual development and accessing what had proved to be an endless, bottomless, limitless ocean of wisdom and understanding of anything I could lay my mind on. The only boundaries it seemed were defined by my own mind.

I had well and truly learned that the quality of all answers is governed by the quality of the questions. And now I could pursue this self awareness with little distraction in the relative anonymity of this breathtaking, invigorating place.

In Hong Kong I achieved something particularly important though, something I'd never managed before. There in the most foreign and unusual place I'd ever experienced, I actually felt at home. Totally at home. Yet I was also aware of being a complete stranger, part of a racial minority, an illiterate.

The foundation for my sense of belonging lay in the sheer energy or 'feel' of the city, certainly, but more significantly from the people I found there and the activities I became immersed in, the vast majority of which related directly to my spiritual development and experiences. I'd truly found another life, not just another me in the same old movie.

It was as though I'd died and rebirthed without losing consciousness. I had all the benefit of accumulated hindsight and awareness as well as the opportunity to put it to practice; to severely edit what I did, why I did it, and how and when... and to learn from it.

This was my introduction to genuine responsibility—personal responsibility for all my actions and undertakings. Every seed I planted would grow or die by my own choice. And I knew it. I'd gotten so used to being part of a system that'd smugly support anyone who wanted to fall back into its homogenous mass-consciousness arms if everything went belly up. I was free. I was also absolutely accountable. I loved it.

As time progressed, people in this new life of mine began to know this 'other' side of me—the spiritual seeker. Some encouraged me to become more openly active in the arena of spirituality and Hong Kong was a place that enabled anything to happen if there was truly a call for it.

Though tolerant and truly benevolent in its own ways, this city would not suffer fools gladly. Well, not for long. If anyone did anything that was truly not supporting others or providing some value, it just died, evaporating into the nooks and crannies of this raw place never to be seen again.

Encouraged by friends to go public with my inner work, I eventually found myself running spiritual development and meditation groups. People were interested. What's more, the interest grew, it didn't evaporate.

Reassured by the support I'd received, I next agreed to run meditation and channeling evenings at the New Age Shop in Central Hong Kong, four Monday nights in a row. They'd be open to anyone who was interested.

I remember the desperately distressing lead-up to those evenings as if it were yesterday. I had to get from my office across Hong Kong in rush hour to the venue, get out of corporate mode and into 'meditation facilitator and channeler' mode to face however many people had decided to turn up. The number varied from only a few to a few dozen, but on the forth night it was a full house. What had started off as my agreement to run only four consecutive Monday evening events became a commitment to continue with the meetings every week thereafter.

Monday nights at The New Age Shop in Hong Kong encouragingly (and frighteningly, I hasten to add!) saw any number of people show up for guided meditations I was running. Following the meditation each evening I drifted into my euphoric quiet time of 'not all there' during which beings of Higher Consciousness would transmit through my voice and body, energy plus wisdom and clarity on people's direct questions for all present to experience and benefit from.

Monday night meditation and channeling evenings at The New Age Shop continued until I eventually left Hong Kong permanently. My leaving authenticated my new commitment to facilitate people's growth, spiritual awareness and empowerment through workshops, seminars and personal private sessions. This work now constitutes my full time occupation in dozens of countries the world over.

Along the way I'd also met Alexandria, the amazing woman who is now my wife, and the latter Monday nights at The New Age Shop in Hong Kong became the first experiences of sharing this work with this soul equally committed to the enlightenment and empowerment of others for the emergence of a new and fulfilling world for one and all.

It had been a fantastic, unbelievable journey of relentless expansion—uncertainty, ecstatic realizations, unexpected upheavals and painful clarity—astounding disruptions associated with the acquisition of self knowledge and the authentic transformation of obsolete dogma and obsession with limitation.

The reward, though, far outweighed the cost.

I knew love. Not only the love of a woman and partner but Love—the capital L variety; Higher Love, Divine Love. And despite the day-to-day disturbances, pains and uncertainties of the continuing process of conscious expansion, I remain blissfully happy in life and feel a sense purpose that I never dreamed possible.

I'd opened to life and all its potentiality, risked my comfort zones and had them shattered repeatedly, and found more of myself than I'd ever dared hope for. I was free. Not free from—free to.

WAKE UP TIME

It had become abundantly clear to me that we all have our own irrefutable connection to the source of all existence and the vast array of potentiality that it confers. I'd learned that this direct connection is, has always been, and always will be solely under our own jurisdiction.

Furthermore, that connection is perpetually there, offering each of us the opportunity to become a potent unique channel for healing and creativity, inspiration and evolution on all levels, at all times. This gift is yours and mine, never to be revoked or compromised unless we allow that to happen.

Whenever you choose, you alone can deepen, strengthen and clarify your own connection to the source of all existence without anyone's permission or blessing. Your natural connection is yours to wield and to master; to use as your own source of all life and life potential.

Everyone has this connection, though in many instances it has been denied or forgotten, discouraged through delusion or buried in bigotry, rendering it less and less accessible and useable... forgotten.

Those transformative times in Hong Kong taught me another vital Truth: whether they're a saint or a sinner, a banker or a beach bum, *everyone* is spiritual. No exceptions.

Every single thing any person does is a part of their own spiritual path, whether or not they realize it or acknowledge it. When they're willing to see and accept this fundamental understanding of their existence, they can immediately begin to develop, refine and utilize its potent effects throughout their day-to-day life by healing all that has ever stood between them and their absolute self power to create and experience whatever they choose. As soon as they acknowledge and begin exercising that inner power of choice, their entire life is able to come into alignment with the unseen network of immutable loving, supportive forces by which we're all bound whether we know it or believe it or like it... or not.

The more thoroughly you open to higher energy and employ natural Cosmic Law throughout your life, the more you'll effortlessly attract joy, abundance, wellbeing, opportunity, peace and love.

This isn't some ability reserved for only a few special people, it's natural for one and all. I've learned without any shadow of doubt that absolutely anyone can bring these attributes into their life.

In fact, that's one thing we're all supposed to do because it is through that function that higher consciousness becomes present on our Earth. All it takes is some awareness of it plus a little self discipline, courage and trust. An unrelenting desire to grow and live one's potential will help, but that'll also develop automatically as one increasingly surrenders to the process of surrendering to growth by opening to life.

What amounted to a series of intense spiritual wake up calls through those transformational years, my own life has revealed to me not theories but a practical understanding of genuine personal growth, evolution and empowerment.

Many years since spent studying the consciousness and lives of real people through my teaching, spiritual counseling, healing and traveling around the world have refined and stabilized the essentials of my understandings, honing them into practical tools for authentic, pan-consciousness transformation.

I know without the faintest shadow of doubt their genuine power since I've experienced them myself, as well as facilitated and observed in countless others the world over, the awakenings I share with you in these pages.

Figure 1

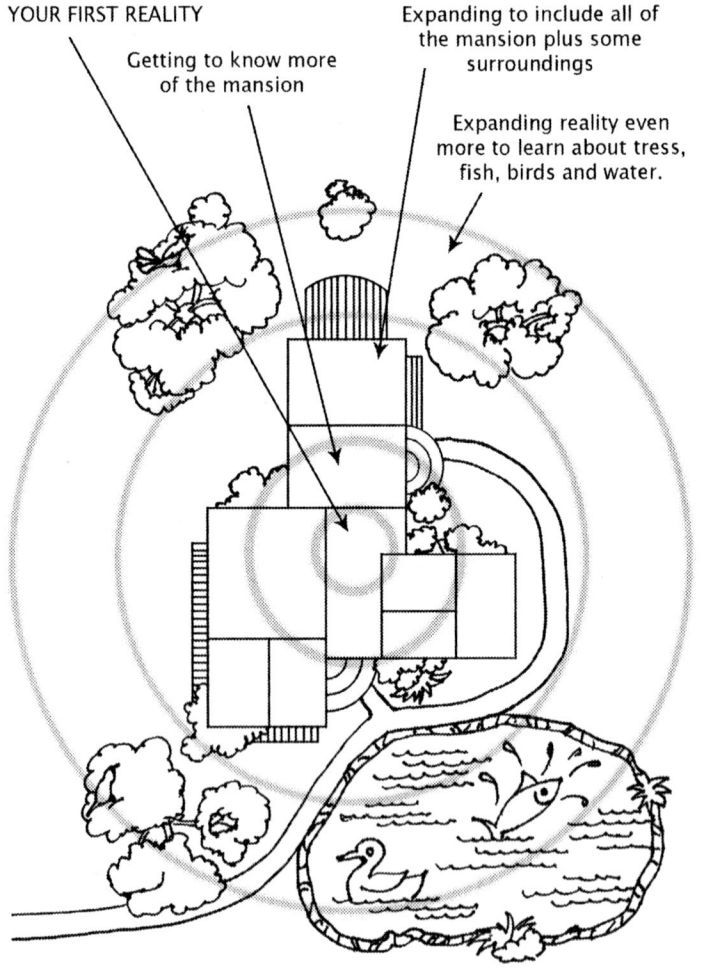

YOUR FIRST REALITY

Getting to know more
of the mansion

Expanding to include all of
the mansion plus some
surroundings

Expanding reality even
more to learn about tress,
fish, birds and water.

GROWING BUBBLES

When I first met Mandy's meditation group in New Zealand, my view of life and everything I believed to be real was painted inside the walls of my own little sphere of convention and predictability.

As I moved on from my encounter with Michael at the jetty, my boundaries were pushed and pulled persistently so that later I'd be able to appreciate what entered my life during those Hong Kong days.

For an appreciation of how this growth-through-uncertainty works, imagine that you're inside a bubble. This bubble contains everything in your life. You were born in this bubble and you know nothing outside its contents. It is your world. All that's within the bubble is your personal reality—your awareness of life and of your potential life experiences.

You're aware only of what's within your bubble and at the farthest horizon of your reality is its inside surface—a mirror, faithfully reflecting back to you everything that you believe to be real; the point at which your view of life ends.

This bubble represents the extent of your present consciousness where your personal view and understanding of your life meets the actual infinite, limitless potential that truly exists.

Now imagine that your bubble is a tiny sphere inside a beautiful big room. You're still conscious only of what's inside your bubble, yet it constitutes only a small portion of the room's contents. It's all that's real to you; it's your reality. But most of the room's contents and space are still outside your bubble's surface.

Furthermore, the room is actually inside a beautiful mansion with exquisite gardens, rich in exotic flora and fauna. The house, its gardens and surrounding countryside are the potential that life actually has on offer, potential that's unlimited, reaching further into the distance than you can see or even imagine. Out there are experiences of innumerable things that don't even occur to you simply because they're not within your bubble.

Now imagine your bubble's skin is of a special substance that lets things pass through it without any damage. This special skin will allow your bubble to expand and stretch as far as you're willing to allow it into the outer potential. Now your reality bubble begins to grow.

Your sphere of consciousness expands and, as new things penetrate its skin and become apparent, you gradually become conscious of more of the infinite potential that's available to you outside. All manner of things that were unknown to you appear through the surface so that inside your bubble there becomes more and more newness for you to explore and experience; more for you to integrate with what you had thought was the limit of realness in your world.

Just like a balloon being inflated, your bubble gradually grows to contain the whole house. You become able to choose which room to be in and when, as gradually all of the rooms become contained inside your reality bubble. *(Figure 1.)* You can now move between the different rooms at will and adjust and rearrange the contents of the rooms to make your new reality the way you want it.

In the same way air inflates a balloon, more and more life support nourishment is filling your bubble to sustain the expansion. The life support nourishment enables you to continue, ensuring that the space inside your expanding bubble doesn't outgrow the sustenance you have. If it did, the sustenance would be too sparse and you'd become unconscious, unable to experience and appreciate the newness that enters your expanding sphere of awareness.

This expansion enables you to become increasingly free from previous limitations and constraints— boundaries you were not even aware you had.

Previously you might have believed that you'd never be able to afford to travel, for example, but you find now in your life of expanded options that the company you've worked for is taken over by a multinational. They determine that you happen to be the best qualified or experienced for some function that is important to their future growth. You suddenly find yourself being sent to other countries to apply your skills and are paid handsomely to do so.

Alternatively, you may have been without a relationship, but as your reality bubble expands it allows in someone you'd never dreamed of, someone who couldn't previously 'get through' your boundaries, and now you're faced with integrating a loving relationship into your usual life pattern.

More and more though, you sense and realize that life becomes an endless supply of newness which you can experience, integrate, change and explore as you choose, by your own free will; an adventure into the true potential of life that, if you're open to it, is never ending—limitless.

I'd love for you to start looking differently at your own reality bubble and to step outside the small portion of your potential to which you've become accustomed, happily or not.

When you can look at your life in an expansive way and objectively study and evaluate with an open mind all that's in your reality, seemingly miraculous things begin to happen. Things that have limited your personal bubble of life experience to date become remarkably clear to you.

"Aha! Now I can see that I've actually been so disdainful and cynical about relationships that I've locked any healthy one out of my life." Or maybe "Oh, now I see that I've been inflexible and resistant to changing my routine that I've disabled myself from getting a new job." Such self awareness and clarity inspires you to explore and apply fresh methods of expanding your experience of life so that you can live and relish more of your infinite potential that's awaiting your pleasure and delight.

"Oh, I think from now on I'll start opening my mind to unlikely possibilities and start believing I can receive some of the limitless potentiality, comforted in the knowledge I can choose whatever I want out of all that exists and all that creation presents to me."

THAT'S LIFE

Obviously, we humans are a part of all that exists. More specifically though, we're the part that's learning what it's like to experience living in physical form and expressing through it.

We're all here on this planet in physical bodies initially to explore what it's like to live in ignorance of the absolute command we actually have over our entire world of experiences. Beyond that, though, our objective is to experience what it feels like to consciously rise out of that ignorance and sense of powerlessness; to deliberately and knowingly regain total awareness of our boundless power and wisdom once more.

In the overall scheme of our spiritual journey into power and wisdom, whether we're happy or sad, successful or unsuccessful, rich or poor, brilliant or simple, beautiful or plain and the like is not actually important. Such qualities are just some of the infinite *potential* ways we might choose to experience life in physical form.

Though we may know in theory that life's potential is limitless, we nevertheless are limited in the ways we actually experience it. No matter how much we might try to convince ourselves that we're not, all of us are experiencing limitation in some way, to a greater or lesser extent.

Your reaction to that notion may be "No! I'm not limited; I know I can be or do anything" but that attitude still remains in your mental world only as a thought or belief. It's not actualized. That is to say, it has not become real in your physical world for you to see, touch, smell, taste and hear. It has not become your actual life experience and is therefore not available for you to tap into, to use or refer to as a true experience.

Cars were a keen interest of mine in earlier years. I joined a car club so that I could pit my driving skills against others on a properly prepared circuit where everyone was racing in the same direction. When I first joined the club I believed without doubt that I was just as capable as the next person of driving fast and well. When I actually raced though, I found that I was not. I had to learn new skills and awareness to actually drive the way I'd been assuming I could. I had to train my skills at the human body's physical, nervous and emotional levels to attain the real ability I'd only believed in my mind I had.

Look at yourself and your own life for a moment. You'll see that some form of limitation exists for you too. Are you able to be as happy, strong, healthy, rich, knowledgeable, popular, fast, skillful, calm, secluded, wise, brilliant, satisfied and fulfilled as you want? Right now? In this instant? If not, then that's a limitation you're experiencing. Can you be in more than one place at one time if you want or need to be? If not, then that's another limitation.

Your mind can *think* of such things, even believe them, but you can't actually experience them. You might say that some ideas can't be classed as limitation since they're just impossible, but it's only your belief about what's possible that creates in you such a limitation.

What you believe is possible and what a person in some primitive civilization thinks is possible are likely to be two vastly different things. Where you draw your boundaries and they draw theirs will not be the same because of your experiences.

You might believe man can travel to the moon but to an uneducated tribe in some ancient culture the mere thought of it might be absolutely ludicrous fantasy, if indeed they could grasp the idea at all. You might even be considered mad for suggesting such a preposterous idea. Vastly different beliefs, yet each belief is as true and real to each person as to the other.

The mind's viewpoint differs from your physical experiential world, bound by the ideas and understandings you believe to be real and meaningful.

These ideas and understandings often seem quite concrete, though they exist on a rather flimsy foundation—that of your own past experiences, your present state of mind and self image, and the ideas, attitudes and beliefs you hold about what's possible, all of which are totally subjective and personal to you; a combination of influences and guidelines by which nobody else but you can or does mould their life.

If you've experienced money and support as effortless resources then your attitude towards, say, starting a new business would be totally different to the attitude of someone with the same business opportunity but who'd only known struggle, isolation and poverty throughout their past.

What's more, the actual success of the business would be different in each case as a result of those differing attitudes and their inherent expectations.

Whatever you've not actually experienced but your mind tells you is possible, constitutes thoughts and beliefs that are not real to you, they're just ideas of real. They remain intangible concepts of potential reality, as long as the belief is not authenticated in physical experience by putting ideas into real action.

A primitive culture may think it's limited to traveling by land, and may vehemently defend that view if challenged. Anything else would seem to them to be a ridiculous assertion. But others believe that flight or sailing are quite normal everyday events.

In such ways, limitation determines what our existence *seems* to be. The way we go about doing life just confirms our beliefs in a tangible material way; our beliefs seem valid because of the *real* confirmation we experience. We've become so accustomed to limitation ruling our lives that we think it's normal; that we have little or no other choice in what we might experience.

What of the mass of population who believed that they'd fall off the edge of the Earth if they sailed over the horizon? What if nobody had ever felt strong enough or free enough from self limiting beliefs to challenge such boundaries in a physical, experiential way? What if nobody had ever gazed at the moon and actually contemplated going there? What if no one had ever wondered how to communicate over vast distances or to travel to far away places?

The simple act of wanting something you don't

have illustrates that you're limited in your ability to have it. Even if you can have it later, you're still limited by time—you can't have it right now.

If you have an illness and would rather be well, then you're limited in your ability to experience the state of health you desire. If you've ever wished you could be relaxing at home instead of being stuck in that traffic yet again, then you're limited in your ability to experience whatever you truly want, whenever you want it.

The whole of our physical existence is based on limitation, albeit in a form and combination of limitations that's unique to each of us. One thing that is unlimited is the possible ways limitation can manifest!

In our realm of limitations, we learn about what it *feels* like to be limited; the pains, frustrations, losses, conflicts, disappointments, powerlessness, lacks, fears, needs and other associated sensations. So that we may come to know and actualize (*real*-ize) our limitations, we also experience their opposites in some way from time to time, feeling what it's like to have, do, be and experience exactly what we want: joy, satisfaction, health, love, power, companionship, strength, comfort and so on.

Though they may be fleeting, these are the moments when we feel empowered. It's through the contrast of these sorts of feelings that we're able to become so convinced that the painful polarity exists, that it's totally real and normal... in fact, that we *must* have it.

How often have you heard or said the words "I can't do that" or "It's impossible" or "That always happens to me"? Such ideas are not true, they're just what we've become convinced are true.

But it's for a very empowering reason. Only by becoming so convinced could we create vividly enough the opportunity and motivation to know the sublime ecstasy derived from emerging out of that state of helplessness—releasing our ignorance of our higher nature and sense of powerlessness in order to reclaim our true power as self acclaimed limitless souls creating in this physical realm.

Empowerment is our biggest lesson... and gift. It comes through feeling what it's like to emerge out of *dis*empowerment—powerlessness and limitation. It's that emergence that creates the sense of liberation, joy, excitement, love, happiness, health, wisdom, inspiration, abundance, purpose—all the wonderful and enlivening feelings derived from rising out of difficulties and shedding unwanted circumstances. I'm sure we've all experienced that relief to some extent, in some way at some time.

In order to experience the powerful positive emotions that arise out of the emergence from limitation, a person must first be engulfed in limiting circumstances. Moreover, those circumstances must be so convincing that they seem real and normal, so overwhelming that nothing else seems possible. The person must become utterly convinced that the limitations are real before they can truly feel what it's like to shed them. If they're not first convinced totally then the whole experience becomes like an act—not real—and the emotions generated become not-real as well; just an act.

The actual form the circumstances take doesn't matter in the slightest, as long as coming out of them generates the deeply authentic positive, elevating, liberating and empowering feelings. Rising from abject poverty into riches, such as a pauper being given a huge sum of money, is an adjustment that would likely generate such powerful feelings of relief, joy and gratitude.

All strong feelings are, in a sense, addictive because by them we know we're alive. Especially positive feelings. We naturally long for them so much that we'll go to any lengths to experience their uplifting influences again. And again and again. That's why we've all been here in life... to experience them.

It also illustrates that the attributes of the experience—good or bad, beautiful or ugly, right or wrong—don't really matter. Ultimately what matters is that we've experienced falling into bleak, often hopeless situations and found our way out again. And the bleaker the circumstances the more intensely joyous, inspiring and uplifting has been the rising out!

Humankind has taken this seesaw life of polarity to the point where many people create for themselves the most extreme circumstances in order to register the most intense feelings... just to know what it's like; just to get the 'buzz'. Take the person who creates painful conflict with their lover just so that they can experience the joyful bliss of making up again... and again and again...

Our souls have undoubtedly lived lifetimes of great variety in order for each of us to know the spectrum of possible experiences and their associated sensations. Each lifetime has been completely separated in our own minds and awareness by the death experience.

Division by death ensured that the experiences within any given lifetime were as pure and potent as possible, undiluted by any other influences or memories of their opposites which would have contaminated the feelings.

For example, if you wanted to deeply understand what it was like to be in absolute poverty, it obviously would not be possible if you were to mix it with an experience of wealth; they're conflicting, mutually defeating circumstances. Like oil and water, they simply don't mix.

How could you truly experience the exhilaration and joy of rising out of poverty and into riches if you knew all along in the back of your mind that you had a huge stockpile of cash sitting in a bank just in case; a safety net that you knew you could rely on if the going got too tough? How could you truly appreciate wealth if you never knew poverty, or vice versa for that matter? No, you'd deny yourself the very experience you set out to create for yourself in the first place; you'd defeat your own purpose for being.

It may seem a little ridiculous that we'd choose such undesirable experiences as poverty, pain, punishment, lack, war, torture, disfigurement, hatred, disablement and disease, but in truth they have no intrinsic value at all. In fact often, by vigorously denying ourselves one attribute in life, we've been able to fully appreciate and put our energy into thoroughly understanding another.

A blind person comes to mind whose hearing is astonishingly acute, far more so than any person with all senses intact, and their appreciation of music is expanded to ecstatic proportions.

Still, all of them are just experiences. They're absolutely neutral until a human puts a judgment upon them. Only by human judgment does any experience become wrong, bad or negative. Such judgments as good or bad and right or wrong are not the way the experience *is*, they're just the way a person *believes* it is. It's simply their personal view of the circumstances, a view prejudiced by their own accumulated experiences and attitudes from the past—their conditioning, which seems so absolutely real and true in their estimation. One person's pleasure is another person's pain; one's medicine is another's poison.

If you personally see someone in any circumstance that you think is 'wrong' or 'bad' then firstly, before judging it or trying to change or fix it, simply say to yourself "Wow, I'm glad I'm not doing that one!" Then, remember: irrespective of our personal biases and conditioning that we hold so dear to us, absolutely every circumstance is *valid*, if only by virtue of its existence.

It exists; it simply *is*, and as such, it's an experience that has been asked for on some level and created in order for humankind to have a completely rounded understanding and appreciation of the overall experience of life. All of it is simply the experience of an unlimited spiritual intelligence practicing limitation through physical form.

The experience doesn't have to be prolonged, but

the souls involved may well have chosen on a higher level to embed themselves very deeply in it to get big evolutionary and spiritual dividends when they emerge.

If for no other reason, it's imperative to always allow people their experiences, at least until they ask for help; and when they do, to assist them not in terms of the experience being eradicated but in terms of helping them realize and eradicate the aspects of their consciousness that are at the source of the experiences they have manifested for themselves.

That is causal cure rather than the usual symptom-tinkering. Otherwise we're being spiritually irresponsible and interfering in another soul's growth and evolution, a sacred path of which we can't possibly have any true knowledge—only they can. They have chosen the experience, no matter how unbearable or wrong it might seem to an onlooker, or even to themselves.

Only they have the right and the ability to get past the circumstances, to experience and feel the exhilaration of emerging out of their powerlessness and into their power once more. If you or I were to do it for them, it would simply guarantee that they'll create the lesson again, only many times more intense, until theyrealize they must deal with it themselves. That is genuine spiritual learning; until the person has achieved it themselves they cannot move on. When they do then all associated trauma, pain and difficulty effortlessly dissolve.

But why would someone put themselves through such hardships and heartaches? First let me say that in order to achieve this limited and limiting type of expression called physical, we had to forget part of ourselves. A very, very large part. In fact the majority. We had to forget our true spiritual nature by becoming ignorant of our natural limitless power and intelligence. We had to relinquish our full awareness of the vital part we each play within all of creation. We had to forget that we're capable of creating whatever we want to experience at any time we choose.

Why forget all this? Simple—you can't genuinely believe you're limited if, at the same time, you have the knowledge that you're not limited! It would be a farce and a waste... and the Cosmos wastes nothing.

In choosing to experience physical versions of ourselves, we earn an immeasurable and unparalleled gift. This reward can be experienced physically but can only be earned spiritually and no other way, no matter what else we might choose to do in the entire scheme of unlimited creation.

The gift is ecstasy, nirvana, bliss, heaven—the unimaginable euphoria and sense of love and liberation that arises from *re*-discovering our true nature as cosmic beings with no limits of any kind.

Wouldn't you handle your life differently if you knew without any shadow of doubt that absolutely nothing lay outside your ability to achieve, have, be and do; that nothing was beyond your experience, if you so chose it?

In common polarity consciousness, which can only be experienced in the dense physical state, we've learned by experiencing opposites—polarities. We came to know the sensation of happiness by making sure we knew the experience of misery in every convincing, vivid detail.

Only by the experience of its polar opposite can we fully appreciate and understand the unique gift of any feeling or experience; only then can we have some way of knowing fulfillment and of understanding, measuring and valuing it.

How can we know and appreciate the heights of joy unless we've fallen to the depths of true sorrow? Or the power of love without having been crushed under the weight of hatred and fear? How can we know what it is to feel free if we've never been incarcerated or felt trapped in some way? How can we truly appreciate and value companionship if we've never felt lonely?

All we've learned to appreciate in life has only been possible by knowing the experience of its polar opposite. We've only known happiness through its polar twin, desperate misery.

How can you gauge, define or understand happiness if it's all you've ever experienced? You'd have no way to evaluate it, no yardstick by which to measure it. How could you even identify that it was actually happiness that your were experiencing?

For this reason, even when they appear to have every conceivable thing that you'd imagine would ensure fulfillment, some people become unhappy or discontented with life. It's why so many people create drama and conflict in otherwise perfectly good relationships—so that they can experience the pleasure of finding love once again; they love *falling* in love rather than *being* in love, because being in love perpetually doesn't generate the same 'rush' of new feelings. Others become angry, bitter or malicious, even violent, just so that they can fall in love again... and feel those feelings.

They've become bored. Their circumstances have become meaningless to them since they feel they can't appreciate or *experience* their happiness and love in a meaningful way any more. They no longer *know* it; they find no way to actually identify it or to feel it since they don't value it any more; they feel nothing by which to gauge it or evaluate it. Why? Because they don't recall what it was like to be without love; what it was like to lack affection, respect and caring. What was life like without such companionship?

There are those who thrill seek while others who, though all their lives seem to have everything, become disenchanted and do astonishingly self hurting and self sabotaging things. Why? Because if they have never known misery, true happiness will be unattainable. If you've never known disease, then chances are you'll not appreciate your good health. Without the threat of death, how will you recognize any opportunity to truly appreciate the gift of life?

People forget. They forget experiences in their past, often the very circumstances that enable them, by sheer contrast to their present situation, to feel Now as strongly as they do. The forgetfulness insidiously undermines people's clarity to the extent that they don't even realize what they have until they have it no more.

Only a wise and objective view of present circumstances can correct the misperception. But the gift of wisdom can be imparted only when you stop, be calm and look past the transient feelings and dramas in your life with a deep and honest intention to understand the Truth—not your personal self-interested truth but the Absolute Truth that pervades all moments, waiting to be discovered and harnessed in liberation and self realization—yours.

Absolute Truth is the Truth that never wears out and never yields to a human ego that becomes bored, irritated, demanding or needy; the Truth that's the unshakeable cornerstone of existence at all levels, transcending human frailties, preferences and perceptions.

When you're willing to accept the idea that, in order to know you're alive you've unwittingly relied upon an addiction to emotional energies coursing through your body, you'll begin your next most important phase—consciously, deliberately refining your growth into Self Power.

All the richness of the love, power, truth and wisdom intrinsic in each moment will begin to be revealed to you as you surrender to the Truth. You'll become increasingly at peace in the knowledge that everything is actually as it's meant to be in every moment. Furthermore, you *"will see the need, as well as the Power, to change your ways and to draw yourself into alignment with Cosmic Law"* (Master Saint Germain).

As the big picture of spiritual growth and evolution—individual and collective—is brought to your awareness and the purpose of humankind's present transformative phase of expansion and spiritual maturity becomes apparent, you'll begin genuinely and thoroughly opening to life.

THE BIG PICTURE

It's over. The Supreme Mind, or boundless Cosmic Intelligence of which we're all a part, is now beginning to make it known to us that all of our learning through the experience of polarities is done; it's complete.

No longer must we experience the dark in order to appreciate the light; nor pain in order to know pleasure. As a species, humankind has actually accumulated all the knowledge we can of these things on behalf of the parent consciousness.

The Supreme Mind now knows so much more of itself. Nevertheless, as indicated by the basic human fear of physical death and our rash assumption that to leave this physical realm is somehow a disadvantage, we don't want to let go of the challenge yet.

A number of influences still convince us to want to continue on this course. Besides the 'pleasure/pain' emotional seesaw, the influences are based on what might be called amnesia.

One is that life as we've come to know it has just been a task we set ourselves but forgot that, like any task, it would eventually be completed. It has become such an automatic way of being; a habit that we can't bear the idea of replacing it, even with something superior.

Another is that we don't remember all of the experiences we've had. Lifetimes separate one set of experiences (called a past life) from another (called Now, for example) so that knowledge of our past has become lost in vast tracts of time and smothered by distractions of present experiences. Consequently, we long to have experiences that we have in fact already had, the memories of which are hidden in the deepest corners of our consciousness, stored in the cells of our bodies as long-term or cellular memory.

Yet another cause is our inability to see ourselves as a unified body of beings (humankind) serving a single higher purpose with the collective body having experienced all things over all time, though the individual parts may not have. When you experience music for example, your foot might experience it by tapping but your hair or your nose probably weren't directly involved in that experience of music. Your body has an overseeing consciousness that doesn't bother that the nose didn't smell music since the experience of music has still been had.

Unlike humans, each like a cell of the body of humankind, whose petulant little egos have the attitude "Yes but *I* want (or don't want) to have that experience too; why does he/she have it and not me?" But as one body of consciousness accumulating the total life experience, together we actually do have the knowledge of the experience we long for, though another person gathered it, not us. And the reverse is also true, that you or I experience what no other has or can; that's the beauty and value of uniqueness.

Uniqueness and variety within our species though seems to generate fear and animosity instead of celebration. Until we see ourselves as being non-separate, a unified species with a common spiritual purpose to reclaim full awareness of our higher nature and cosmic essence, the self interested *me too* desire will plague us and our world with the curse of control and the futility of judgment, both hopelessly misguided byproducts of our addictive ego polarity seesaw.

Probably the most significant is the addiction we have to the roller coaster ride of life. Without even knowing it, the individuals of our human species (and therefore the species itself) are obsessed with bouncing from one emotional extreme to the other; it's the thrill of feeling that we're alive. We're hooked on life, or at least our present picture of life, to the extent that most people will go to extraordinary lengths to create drama, extremes, disappointments, failures and all manner of negative situations just so that they can go for the opposite thrill... and get it.

We've consistently created for ourselves the experience of one polarity so that we can long for and regain the other, just to feel and know the euphoria of emerging out of negativity, pain, struggle and limitation.

What started out as a heartfelt longing for awareness has eventually created desires, needs, cravings—obsessions of all kinds. These in turn have grown to occupy our minds and awareness to the exclusion of everything else. That is to say, everything except the polarized physical world; the world of the senses that appear now to be the *source* of fulfillment, instead of simply the source of life experience and of the wisdom and self awareness to be discovered therein. Events and circumstances are not experience, our response to them are our experience.

However, in stepping back for a moment and taking the overview, we'll see that this has actually been a training course. A severe one, granted, but only practice, nevertheless.

The human craving to satisfying desires, needs and addictions has been like an apprenticeship for the big one—the return to full awareness again from the state of ignorance; to nirvana from suffering—self realization and conscious inner power totally restored.

In this wider picture, all of our accumulated past experiences play a vital role. Rising repeatedly out of some sort of suffering into a sense of joy would eventually create a powerful longing, as well as the energy to fulfill it; a kind of spiritual momentum.

Like a great tide, it's an impelling force that was programmed into our spiritual journey to well up when

Figure 2

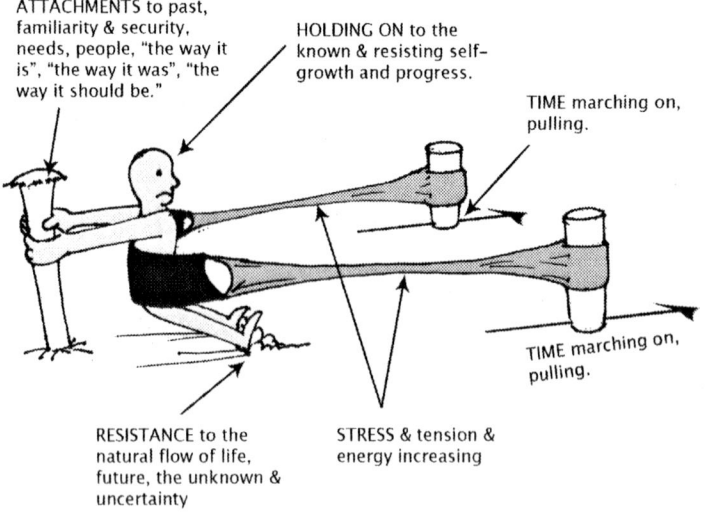

ATTACHMENTS to past, familiarity & security, needs, people, "the way it is", "the way it was", "the way it should be."

HOLDING ON to the known & resisting self-growth and progress.

TIME marching on, pulling.

TIME marching on, pulling.

RESISTANCE to the natural flow of life, future, the unknown & uncertainty

STRESS & tension & energy increasing

our real task was complete and carry us back home with our gathered experiences. It serves as a surge of consciousness energy that we could apply to our self realization when we'd done it all; when there was nothing else left to apply it to in our dense physical realm except wasteful repetition... or... a catapult into the next phase of the journey.

Using our life experiences as springboards, this gigantic energy now enables us, with assistance from higher orders of intelligence inherent in that energy, to reclaim our limitless potency by means of our regular world of experiences; to create our spiritual rising; our ascension into a higher plane of existence, a higher state of being... whilst in a body, on Earth.

Think of it as a spiritual slingshot. The flow of time and our evolution marching on relentlessly is akin to pushing forward the arms of the slingshot to create tension to harness increasing power. *(Figure 2)*

The hand holding back the shot is the fundamental human addiction to the belief that we're bound to exist by the laws of life and death; of fear, limitation and polarity and all of their effects. The tensioning rubber is our emotional attachments to the status quo—the trials and tribulations of polarity consciousness to which we've grown so addicted.

As the tension increases with the march of time, so does our sense of stress and urgency to 'do something' or rethink our lives, beliefs and priorities, spurred by our unconscious knowing that The Time has come. The shot itself is, of course, us—humankind; you and me.

When our obsessions and perceived needs

(emotional attachments) to maintain our present form of polarity- and conflict-based existence are dissolved and harmonized (healed), it will release the tension contained in our slingshot and we'll be propelled forward with unimaginable impetus into a love- and harmony-based existence involving not exclusive power—that of domination and control—but mutual power; not power over anyone but instead power within all of us; power *to*...

Our spiritual momentum is thus fuelled by the energy released when we dissolve our obsession with polarity, competitiveness and conflict (the "If I don't first, they will" mentality) and our preoccupation with needing to accept and preserve, even satisfy, the status quo (the "Be nice, don't make waves" mentality).

It's a little like a new lease on life... the energy we find when we're offered an ideal new job after being unemployed; or when we encounter a wonderful new lover after an abusive or toxic relationship, or a period of paralyzing, hopeless loneliness.

This is the purpose and the path of self realization. When a person has become ready to move on from just playing around with creating and experiencing the fleeting pleasures of physical life, they naturally begin to think there must be something more permanent, meaningful and fulfilling into which they can grow. They begin their spiritual awakening as a result. This is not to the exclusion of those fleeting pleasures but instead to keep them in perspective so that they no longer rule one's life, oneself does.

Again taking the overview, the present situation

is that humankind has collectively reached that point. In subtle or evident ways, through these years surrounding the passing of the old and the arrival of the new millennium, everyone is awakening to the futility and obsolescence of much of the world as it has been.

Many are saying "It just can't happen this way any more; it doesn't work" or "There's got to be another way, another solution" without having the faintest idea what that solution might be. Their apprenticeship is served and they're now beginning to get the spiritual message by way of a calling from deep within. It may not make any sense at first but it is there, stirring them deep within.

In even the most mundane moments people are beginning to awaken to something that's very real to them but most often defies rational reason or explanation. People everywhere in all walks of life are feeling deeply motivated to step out of this intense but obsolete game of polarized experiences, instead seeing the sense in redirecting their efforts in life; discerning the opportunities to apply their longing to greater things—their own self power; awareness of their true wider spiritual nature; rediscovery of their own true cosmically unlimited spiritual intelligence that's fully aware of its connectedness with all of creation and able to consciously choose what it will experience at every moment.

At last people are beginning to release their spiritual slingshots.

The most astonishing thing about this shift in consciousness—something that, remarkably, makes it all worthwhile yet at the same time totally unfathomable—is that we have the opportunity to remain entirely conscious, awake and alert during this reclamation of our spiritual awareness and unbounded cosmic potency.

We're all able to be fully and constantly aware of our unlimited powers of creation as they reveal to us bit by bit, step by step, each new and exciting aspect of our greater existence, our magnificent Higher Self unveiling to our insecure little limited ego self as we go through everyday life. We will now witness the fading of our limited understanding and limiting experiences of life fade as they make way for full time ecstasy, boundless wisdom and unquestionable power throughout all circumstances.

This will prove to be a source of immeasurable rapture, the likes of which we're presently unable to even imagine and the intensity of which will provide enough momentum for us to burst through to our next phase of evolution.

It's as though you've been born and permanently locked in a dark cold dungeon. The environment of the dungeon is all you've known as life. Because it's all you've known, you naturally consider it normal and you've come to believe and evaluate life in terms of cold, hard, damp and lonely, being aware of nothing else.

Now, however, someone has come to the door and is saying "You can come out now." You could be excused for wondering "But what exactly is 'out'—out of what? This is all there is." After all, your cell is all that there is, so what could be 'out there' that could ever mean life?

Your polarity mind would habitually think, "If it's not life as I know it then it must be the opposite—death!" "What can life be outside here where I know it?"

You didn't even realize you'd been 'inside' so how could you have known there was an 'outside' or that life existed there?

Life means what you've personally experienced it to mean, nothing more, nothing less. You take it for granted that sustenance is somehow made available by unseen forces. You didn't even know walls existed—they were just the horizon of everything that had ever meant anything real to you. They were the edge of your reality, the end of your world!

But... what could it be like to have no edge, no limits? If this dungeon is not all that is, then where does that lead to?

Who would be out there? What would they be like, look like? What sort of powers would they have and what could those unimaginable beings do to you? Are they the invisible forces which have somehow sustained your life for all time? Wouldn't that put them in control of your destiny? Maybe this is just some sick joke they're playing. What a helpless, disempowering, even frightening thought!

Are they the ones who created your world in there in the first place and still control its conditions? How will you interact with them? Will they like you, hate you or be quite indifferent? Bring you harm or help? What about getting a new kind of home? What about your loved ones? Your children? Your dreams? Your work? What could it all possibly mean?

Surely it would be easier to just stay in the dungeon, right? It'd be less complicated, less effort. And at least you'd know what to expect. Right?

What will you do with your time 'out there'? For that matter, how will you know what's there for you to do and experience outside if you always believed the dungeon was all that existed?... How will you adapt to the bright light out there? And the wide open space?...

What's it all about? What's going on?

Is the world going mad?

You can only begin to get an idea of the potential magnitude of the quandary—a problem without limits or a benefit without limits?

You see, what I present you with here in these pages is the idea of an emergence into a life, a reality, a world that has the potential and the ability to become new in *every conceivable and inconceivable way*.

The indescribable expanse, choice, light, freedom—the lack of limitation; no walls!—may at first be daunting, not even believable, but then so was Copernicus' idea that the planets revolved around the Sun, not around the Earth as everyone had been believing.

During my double decade career in the creative area of advertising, I both saw and experienced the dilemma, even distress and disarray that can arise from creative opportunities given without rules or guidelines—without a 'brief' as it was called. In that business, prolifically creative people can become dumbstruck, unable to apply their abilities because they're only familiar with a target to aim for or boundaries to work within. I was working with very talented people but they'd never had to decide for themselves what to use their creative abilities on or to take responsibility for them.

As you come to see and experience personally the truth of the new emerging reality, it'll become increasingly real and apparent, even rapturous for you. As you discover more and more of that new world of love, light, freedom, wisdom and mutual powerfulness, it will become more meaningful and experiencable. The new potential will no longer be just potential— intangible, abstract, conceptual, waiting to happen— it'll be real and permanent and meaningful to one and all as real life, a totally new life at that.

Why will this rapture be so profound and lasting? Because humankind has experienced limitation, pain and suffering. We've known intimately the fear that rises out of powerlessness and ignorance to cripple any meaningful sense of personal freedom, creativity, initiative and direction.

We've known and understood these things and we will retain a vivid memory of them like indelible files in the storage system of our consciousness. Indelible but obsolete, they will serve as a constant reminder of our natural magnificence and omnipotence and the immeasurable bliss derived from regaining full awareness of our cosmic nature and reclaiming our power in every moment of our lives, never to feel powerless again.

And we'll continue to grow beyond even those truths, embracing new, more fulfilling ideas of ourselves and our potentiality that will in turn become superseded by still higher truths. We'll carry the understanding and knowledge forward so that the intelligence in other realms of consciousness— alternative aspects of ourselves that have not benefited from the gift of physical experience—can learn from us and know itself more fully and accurately.

That those higher aspects have only ever experienced bliss, cosmic awareness and omnipotence and known nothing less means they can learn from us, further understand their Supreme nature and more deeply appreciate their unique role in the scheme of All Creation.

We stand to contribute a vital step to the Supreme Plan if we're willing to move on from the type of world we've become familiar with into one that'll render all our foundations and beliefs, dramas and obsessions obsolete.

We'll claim an immeasurable gift of enlightenment through being of vital service by opening to life, bathing in its uncertainty and surrendering to the flow of All Creation as it brings us out of darkness and self ignorance into Light—self awareness, love and mastery.

GOING WITH THE FLOW

During a heavy downpour, rain falling on your roof must find a way to the ground so that your home doesn't become flooded. To guide rain from the roof effectively, pipes are fitted. They're channels through which the rain water flows to ground. If these channels get blocked by leaves, twigs or other debris, then your house will inevitably become flooded in a future downpour making it at best uncomfortable or, at worst, uninhabitable.

Your own personal energy system operates in just the same way bringing life force into your body. As a field of energy at various vibrational rates, you consist of your physical body permeated by your subtle, non-physical bio energy field.

This flow takes place by way of a very sophisticated architecture consisting of energy transfer portals (commonly called chakras) and dynamic subtle energy pathways (called meridians) which allow pure life force energy to enable and nourish every part of you.

If you think of life force energy as rain water and your body's energy meridians and chakras as drainpipes, you have the picture: life force energy pouring through your body's energy channels. This mechanism enlivens the otherwise lifeless form of your physical body.

When your energy system is in optimum condition, it enables pure life force energy to flow through you at a maximum rate that's unique and perfect for you. This individual ideal rate ensures that you can be fully alive without ever becoming overwhelmed by the limitless potential of the life force energy.

Through this system, you're able to gain maximum benefit from life throughout your sojourn in the physical dimension. If the life force energy stopped flowing through your physical body, your material form would becomes life-*less*—you'd physically die.

Meridians and chakras are your energetic plumbing. They're channels through which original, unadulterated life force energy actually endows you with life. Further to that somewhat pragmatic healthful function, you are a unit of consciousness which serves as a channel for the intelligence that's within in that life force energy.

Thus, that higher intelligence is able to experience and know life in dense physical form, in contrast to its origins in non-physical dimensions. You could think of it as an idea or thought (non-physical level) which motivates the body to do something (physical level) to demonstrate or enact its idea, thought or intention.

That makes you a channel for higher conscious-ness—essential life force energy; the interdimensional energy of the cosmos from which all life, form and phenomena are created. You're a natural channel for this energy. You're a natural channel for absolutely everything, potentially—all phenomena conceivable and inconceivable, form and formless, sensations and substances, actions and feelings, thoughts and awareness and events. You're an interdimensional facilitator for All That Is!

Just being alive means you serve and contribute to

the creation of absolutely all elements of nature, of humankind, of human nature and of course our planet. You're a natural channel for the flow of fundamental godforce (or whatever other label you might prefer to use for the concept of a Supreme Intelligence or all-embracing being... All That Is, God/Goddess, The Creator, The Cosmic Principle/Principal, The Ultimate Intelligence, The Source).

You're a natural channel for the Divine. There is nothing special or exclusive about it, it's just what you are as well as how and why you exist. You can't stop it, you can only use or abuse it, refine or confuse it, your unique personal blend of which paints a particular picture of existence in a particular slice of the cosmos called... *your life*.

Dictionaries describe a channel as a means of access or communication, or a course along which something moves or flows. Obviously, a narrow, blocked or closed channel compromises or limits the access and the capacity for movement along it; a wide, clear or open channel maximizes it.

It stands to reason that if your energy channels are restricted or compromised in any way, so is your ability to allow higher consciousness to flow through you. However, if your channels are clear and open then your ability to represent the Supreme Cosmic Intelligence is automatically increased, along with your own capacity to live life.

So what blocks a person's energy channels? Primarily, resistance. Resisting life; resisting the uncontrolled, unpredictable flow of creation. The resistance is created by harboring and employing attitudes and beliefs based on fear. Their signs include anger, bitterness and self doubt; conflict and dis-ease; overbearance and dominance and the will to restrict or deny their own or another soul's free will or self power through control or limitation of any kind.

The extent to which you knowingly or unknowingly, intentionally or unintentionally restrict your channels determines the extent to which the flow of life force energy is restricted through you—the extent to which your own life becomes limited or less than ideal. This is due to the fact that the energy *is* life itself. It's the stuff that flows through the channels of your energetic architecture and enables you to be a physical being, conscious of your life in a physical world and creating it all as you go along your life journey.

Some people call this energy prana while others, depending on their race, creed, nationality or religion, refer to it as chi, ki, orgone, pneuma, mana, spirit and various other terms. As with all things in life, any label you give it doesn't alter what it actually is, only what it means to you and how you experience it. Aside from the labels, it's simply the essential energy that's life; existence; consciousness.

It follows then that as a human being you're actually consciousness from higher dimensions (Supreme Intelligence) expressing through your form (body) inside this physical dimension (our world and universe). Your are therefore essentially a purely spiritual being operating through a physical body.

The intensity of energy beyond our physical

dimension is much higher than we can sustain, certainly in life as we presently know it. Therefore, when it enters our dimension to perpetuate life and consciousness, its intensity must be reduced in order to avoid overwhelming us and our world. At the same time, it must become practical, meaningful and useful to us as well as provide a high enough frequency to be inspiring and enlightening.

This must be no mean feat, requiring the energy's frequency to be lowered to myriad levels to resonate more closely with ours, otherwise it would be undetectable and irrelevant to us, not unlike a human trying to hear the pitch of a dog whistle or to see ultraviolet light with the naked eye.

The consciousness enters our dimension of existence through specifically designed channels— us. That's what makes you a channel of the life force energy as well as being the mechanism by which its frequency is lowered to become sustainable in this physical realm of ours. As the energy enters *you* specifically from the higher vibrational levels of Light through the channels of *your* energy system, it becomes translated into *your* life—*your* personal version of reality.

Your personal reality—everything you're person- ally aware of and consider to be real—consists of three levels, or dimensions: physical, emotional and mental. They're the ways you are conscious of life. You're able to relate to life, experience it, feel it, evaluate it, understand it and interact with it mental, emotional and physical means.

Once the energy has entered the individual unit of consciousness that you are, it gradually drops in frequency as it filters down from your higher chakras to the lower ones. Not unlike steam condensing into water, the energy becomes more and more physical as it distributes through first, your subtle mental and emotional energies, then through your electrical and nervous systems, and on through your body chemistry, glands, organs and tissues until finally it expresses into the physical realm through your body as your physical form and the things you do—your own unique life!

Your energy field has innumerable channels to handle this exquisite energy flow. They're the only means by which the flow of life force energy is able to enter and enliven the otherwise lifeless form of your body. If this faculty was lost, disabled or totally blocked, it would result in an absence of life force in your body that would render it life-*less*.

If, instead of becoming completely blocked, the energy just became distorted, congested or polluted so that it didn't flow with ease, then it would bring *dis*-ease to your body. Your body would not reflect accurately the true (natural, higher) nature of the pure energy, instead demonstrating the way you'd corrupted it.

If, on the other hand, you were to clear or open those channels, you'd liberate the flow of pure cosmic life force energy through you. It would flow more easily and intensely, in larger quantities and at higher frequencies. Since that life force energy is the source of who you are and what and how you are being, then surely it follows that by opening your channels you'd naturally become more filled with life as well as being a more accurate representation of the true origins of your life force in higher realms of consciousness.

That being the case, the higher aspects of your consciousness would manifest through you more faithfully in their boundless expressions of love, wisdom and omnipotence—qualities that give access to the abundance, power, joy, love and fulfillment that so many people seek—instead of your lower self in its ego-distorted expressions and addictions, and your belief in you and your life being necessarily limited.

The influx of higher consciousness would transform your whole life into a human demonstration of higher consciousness. You'd become a physical-world manifestation of your Higher Self; a walking talking Earthly demonstration of your God Self.

Hey presto, you become a Divine, spiritual being in a human body. As a result, you get to enjoy and demonstrate to others the extraordinary wisdom, power and joy, and live the limitless abilities and cosmic ideals of the higher dimensions of consciousness—the spiritual realms in which your roots are inextricably entwined throughout eternity.

That's exactly how all the spiritual masters in history contributed markedly to the development of world consciousness in their own unique way, each in their own time and in their own particular way and location on the Earth. They kept their own channels open and clear of blocks—clear of fear and all its insidious manifestations of need, control, domination, self denial and powerlessness.

Their relentless spiritual diligence and discipline enabled those masters to attain and maintain that state of purity and assured them ready access to the immutable Supreme Laws and Truths of the cosmos.

They were guided by a higher spiritual perspective and their lives demonstrated that wisdom and understanding rather than the limited and limiting human versions of understanding life and our potential that prevailed in the societies and civilizations that surrounded them at the time.

Their commitment and discipline gave them the ability to live in a way that seemed outside the human norm. In many instances, even outside the accepted beliefs about human capabilities. They demonstrated skills and attributes of Divine rather than Earthly nature, their words and deeds often so extraordinary that they seemed impossible... which they were, if it weren't for their open channels perpetually invoking the energy of higher consciousness.

Like miracles, they and their feats became etched in people's minds as well as in the annals of history. Though all they did was exemplify Cosmic Truth, these clear channels became idolized through religious doctrine and their wisdom frequently twisted by human fear and control into such social diseases as dogma, war and bigotry which have plagued our history.

In reality their wisdom and feats seemed so miraculous simply because they were so unlike the norm of their day; they were so different and exuded such a different energy, one that might now be called charisma. Through their chakras, their auric fields radiated higher frequencies of energy so faithful to their spiritual Source that they seemed inexplicable; out of context—impossibly out of context in many instances. Some, for example, were reportedly felt passing a town or village when they were actually some distance away, out of visual range.

On a more rational basis, however, they achieved and became what they did just because they established their clear access to the life force energy; they maintained the openness to the absolute potentiality that lies beyond a common human sense and awareness of life.

They were cosmically aware, actualized masters of the Cosmic Laws and spiritual principles and forces that determine and shape all life. They were soul-aligned, self realized beings walking this planet in physical bodies. By shedding their need to be normal and acceptable, actively pursuing higher understandings and allowing their actions to be motivated by their higher inspiration and transcendent wisdom rather than their surrounding influences, these extraordinary people effectively began walking and talking higher wisdoms and qualities that were later labeled 'spiritual.'

They lived and taught according to their own higher truth—the understanding they gained through their own innate connectedness to higher consciousness. In doing so they were able not only to demonstrate these miraculous characteristics but to encourage and inspire masses of people to realize those same qualities in themselves; to see that the same miraculous nature is inherent in all human beings just waiting to be discovered; just waiting to be allowed to flow out through ever clearer channels of the individual fragments of humankind the world over—us; you and me. Their intention was that our species would so enable itself to move to its next phase of power, love and wisdom through enlightenment.

Clearing your channels begins the process of self healing. This involves identifying and consciously dispersing all blocks, distortions and congestion that compromise the flow of life force energy through you. Your energy field has become congested through all previous life experiences like a river suffocated by debris and pollution that has built up through bygone storms and floods.

Debris and pollution in a human body takes the form of energy toxins on the physical, emotional and mental levels. These toxins are caused by low consciousness, fear based attitudes, beliefs, reactions, emotions, habits and activities. Not only have these pollutants brought about disease, they have also compromised your awareness and intelligence by clouding or even disabling your contact with our Higher Self and higher awareness. Their influence has disconnected you from the Truth that you're an omnipotent master of all life.

Suppression is resistance to *ex*-pression. Suppression forces things to stay inside and thus is the root of disease. By trying to force the higher flow to stop, the frequency of the life force energy becomes lowered, suppressed by fear and by resistance to the unbridled expression of one's unique self.

This could be likened to a tap where the water represents the life force energy: if you were to mix flour into the flow coming through the tap it would make the original water thicken like jelly and it would obviously not flow with ease. Similarly, when you mix mental, emotional and physical toxins into the natural flow of life it congests the life force energy and causes disease. Those toxins are your resistances to the natural flow of life and they stem from your own unique, fear based conditioning and biases accumulated from past experiences, circumstances and influences.

Unfortunately, the situation has been that way for so long that most people now believe that they're helpless, or some kind of spiritual minion. Some people even believe they're unspiritual or a spiritual vacuum— a helpless case who needs a guru or master to guide them; who is ignorant and needs a knowing and wise teacher; who is in the dark and needs to be enlightened. But really this is pure self denial.

As is the case with everyone, that wise and all knowing guru and master, as well as the enlightenment sought are already within their life force energy. It's streaming in constantly, direct from a source far higher than any guru on this Earth, just waiting to be discovered and allowed to manifest. It's just that such people are in the habit of suppressing their uniqueness, self belief and self trust.

By seeking acceptance (of family, peers, religions, culture, creed) through uniformity, they block the very consciousness that could set them free from their limited lives. They have severed, or at least severely stifled the flow of the very energy that could enable them to heal physically, emotionally, mentally and spiritually, and thus restore and clarify their natural and eternal connection to the source of their all powerful, all knowing, all seeing God nature within.

This process is ultimately determined by self, not by some guru or priest or other supposed representative of God. Ironically, the Truth will inevitably emerge that they themselves are the representatives of God that they'd been seeking all along. Self denial is all that stands in their way.

Restoring your connection to your soul essence means opening to life force energy; clearing yourself of physical, emotional and mental debris; identifying and discarding what's no more than old obsolete conditioning of the past which serves only to block the flow of your pure Divine nature now and thereby create disease in the future.

The first step in identifying that toxic conditioning is to ignore for a moment what appears to be real and ask yourself "Do my beliefs, attitudes and thoughts concerning life describe to me an image or idea of wellbeing, love, abundance, ease, empowerment and joy?"

Be brutally honest with yourself. If they do not paint a pretty picture of life then it's high time you began adopting beliefs, attitudes and thoughts that do. After all, those mental images are perpetually tinting the flow of life force energy as it passes through you into life; they are the seeds of your entire reality, of your life and all of your circumstances.

What you sow now you shall certainly reap later. So why not do yourself a favor now—sow seeds (hold thoughts and attitudes and beliefs) that'll ensure you'll increasingly reap a supportive and wonderful reality rather than a disappointing or miserable one. It's literally as easy as changing your mind. Take your mental hands off the steering wheel of life, be flexible and let it guide you instead of you steering it.

Remember: Now is the result of everything that has gone before and *your* now is the result of everything *you* have done and been to date. Whether you are happy or not, remind yourself perpetually that continuing on the same regime will only achieve more of the same result.

Allowing yourself to embrace a different attitude will allow you to explore a different life full of different experiences; a life that'll reflect your new choice of attitudes and ideas and beliefs. If you don't like some part of your circumstances, begin to change their source—you—opening your channels by relaxing the demands and influences you hold over the flow of life force energy through you.

The mere intention and act of opening your channels to the flow of unadulterated life force energy through you and into your life is the single most self loving, vital, healing and spiritually responsible contribution you can make to your own enlightenment and sustainable wellbeing. It enables you to be a clearer expression of Divine qualities, firstly for your own healing and realization of self power and mastery, and secondly to exemplify that Divinity to your fellow human beings, demonstrating to them that any human is able to dissolve self limiting beliefs and attain a state of power, love and fulfillment throughout each and every moment and experience of their life.

BLOCK BUSTING

Let's take a closer look at the implications of the fact that absolutely everything you are and everything you experience originates in the flow of life force energy. The consciousness, or energy, descends through your energy system becoming translated into your own personal way of being, your personal consciousness, your life.

It stands to reason that anything you put into the flow upstream (in the higher frequency, non-physical levels) will appear downstream where it comes out (in the physical world). As above, so below. If you were to throw beautiful pink flower petals onto a river upstream then pink flower petals would also appear on the water downstream. The more petals cast on the river, the more will appear downstream. Should the river be winding and cluttered with debris and obstructed by boulders then the chances are that less petals will make the full journey than if the river were straight and clear. Makes sense.

With the energy entering your consciousness 'above' and exiting 'below' like a river, all that stands in the way of the pure Supreme nature of the energy entering your life is... *you*, and how you influence the flow.

Like the river, if your state of being is convoluted and complicated with obstructions to life's natural flow, and clutter of resistance, fear and unhealthy emotions, then it stands to reason that less of the true Supreme nature of the original energy will reach your life. Your life will exhibit less of the qualities of higher frequency consciousness—less love, abundance, harmony, empowerment and fulfillment.

On the other hand, if you align your awareness and everyday way of being with the higher consciousness qualities, opening to their potential to manifest in your life in extraordinary unexpected ways, then the more love, abundance, harmony, empowerment and fulfillment will manifest in your life as the energy enters and flows through you unhindered.

The way you choose to *be* in life and to view life at any given time determines how readily you're able to rise out of limitation and victimhood and become empowered with the extraordinary qualities of mastery—being fully aware of, responsible for and active in your absolute power in every moment of your life.

The way that you're being is your unique expression of consciousness and filters the original energy, flavoring it with your own idiosyncrasies. That could be with your biases, conditioning, preconceptions, negativities, resistances and judgments or through your allowance, sense of fun and adventure, harmonious attitudes and expectation of new and wonderful experiences around every corner on life's journey. Or for that matter, any blend of the two.

The unique blend you're being will invariably be reflected to you in exact, vivid detail as the experiences you're having of life. Therein lies the greatest guidance of all—guidance to true self awareness and real causality in your life.

Depending on their particular quality, each trait either enhances or compromises the ex-pression of your deepest truth and highest potential, in accordance with your beliefs and attitudes towards yourself and life. It's the compromising ones that lower the frequency of the energy in your life by putting controls and conditions on your deepest yearnings.

Such attitudes as "I'd better not upset the peace" or "Someone might not like me doing that" are common examples of self suppression—limitation of the self. These are *inner* conflicts. They never arise unless there was already an unconscious inner urge to do something which conflicts with the self conscious (ego) that wants to appease outer influences. They are a sign that your soul is guiding you, but your ego is stopping you. And it is simply your choice, your responsibility which one you trust and heed.

In the most healthy scenario, people would express themselves fully in words and actions... with poise and compassion. But express themselves fully and truthfully, nevertheless.

In the least healthy scenario one would simply suppress the inner urge, keeping it deep inside by pretending it didn't exist and that there was no inner conflict at all. In such circumstances, the ego influences the flow of consciousness in subtle ways in order to control and mould the flow of life experiences to suit itself. These are the conditioned knee-jerk reactions favored by the ego to preserve your comfort zone—the boundaries of limitation created by your subconscious fears, judgments, resistances and conditioned biases.

Yet these boundaries are completely arbitrary. They're just habits that have been established for no healthy nor rational reason, only to preserve your physical, emotional and mental status quo and that of others around you. They only stop you growing; stop you exploring your potential by keeping you on the same old merry-go-round.

They've formed to protect fragile human egos from each other in a dance of fear, control and suppression—ostensibly, a mutual game of lies, deception and disease, albeit out of sheer habit, with the participants really not realizing it nor its implications.

Children are wonderful examples of the interaction between spontaneity and suppression. Let's say a child runs up to its parent and says "I love you!" and moves to hug them. The parent is talking to a neighbor at the time and politely and patiently says something along the lines of "Yes yes very nice dear, but just wait a moment, I'm talking to someone right now." Immediately, the child learns that it's not always okay to express love spontaneously to the person they love most and who most represents love in their life.

If that child carries a propensity for lessons in expressing love, then that experience becomes a seed of conditioning. In the future, if that child is not given the opportunity or encouragement to show and receive spontaneous love, then from that moment on they'd likely hesitate, albeit for just a split second, to evaluate whether or not it's okay before they express love to anyone, even people who represent love to them. After all, if it's not okay to express love spontaneously to a parent, who is it okay to love?

The hesitancy reinforces the suppression of the

love rather than the expression of it. Every time that conditioning convinces the child to hesitate in any future circumstances, it sends an instantaneous imperceptible ripple of influence through their whole consciousness, restricting their expression of love a little more each time.

Later in life, those ripples can amount to overwhelming emotional tidal waves in everyday situations involving love. The child-now-adult can become so blocked to the flow of love that they may be unable to express love at all to the very people who are closest to them—their lovers, their family, and even to their own children.

That suppression of love becomes the norm for them. They don't even realize they're doing it since it feels so normal to them; so comfortable; the way it's always been. But it creates dis-ease around all experiences of love in their life. As you might imagine, the child grows with that bias and their own child, seeing their dearest loved one—a parent—being ill at ease or non-expressive around issues of love, consequently also learns unconsciously that it must be natural and correct to suppress love.

Such conditioning goes on and on through generations until someone becomes aware of it and has the insight and courage to step outside the comfort zone it supports. Then they'll break that cycle of disease for their entire ancestry.

No sickness or physical condition is hereditary. Beliefs and attitudes are hereditary. I believe without any shadow of doubt that they, not any biological issues, are the cause of all bloodline illnesses, defects and disabilities. Our entire physical form is the product of our higher energies of intention, imagination, attitude, belief and thought. They only reach the energy levels of materiality and circumstance through persistence. So-called hereditary biological disorders and illnesses are actually the product of hereditary beliefs and attitudes handed down through generations. It's the "My father voted conservative so I vote conservative too" mentality; the "If it was good enough for our parents then it's good enough for us" cop out.

Likewise, the social diseases that plague humanity. Halting their relentless march through ongoing generations begins with developing an awareness of damaging beliefs and attitudes—toxic consciousness.

The next step is true healing through teaching and supporting new generations in the disciplines of genuinely enlightened and healthy attitudes and beliefs based on Cosmic Truths, not upholding the rigidity, fear and assumptions of human bias, conditioning and status quo mentality that are perpetrated in the name of education simply to appease fragile human mass-egos. Same mentality, same reality... as far as the eye can see.

Regarding the child and its ongoing love issues, gaining awareness and understanding of these inner influences is therefore the first step towards healing the disease or distortion in their own consciousness as well as in the hereditary conditioning that permeates and surrounds them.

The second step is to introduce the discipline and courage to address and correct the lack of unconditional love being exchanged in their life. That comes about by breaking the mentality mould; by rethinking and repairing their attitudes and responses to circumstances surrounding their unrestricted giving and receiving of love; daring to think and be differently.

Your Higher Self doesn't want you to stop living because if you did then you couldn't fulfill your higher purpose to gather experience in the material world. So it ensures that the life force energy flows relentlessly.

The energy builds up pressure where there is any blockage or resistance to it, like a river that wells up where it encounters a dam. You feel this pressure as your individual measure of the stress of life itself. The quiet but continual trickle of a mountain stream ultimately demands an enormously strong dam to hold back the amassed water. Just as each inner block added creates a higher dam that'll have to withstand a higher pressure from the stream, so each time you suppress the natural flow of the life force in some way, you build a stronger block in your channels that'll have to withstand a higher pressure in exactly the corresponding area of your life.

If it's the unbridled flow of unconditional love you've been blocking or resisting, then love issues will appear to become even more frequent and intense in your life. If it's your fear of public speaking that you've been giving in to then rest assured you'll have plenty of reasons to overcome your resistance in that area, maybe by being spontaneously put on the spot or having demands placed on you relentlessly to deliver your truth.

Blocks and resistance to the natural flow of

life reduce the vibration of the life force energy, compressing it against the blockage until it ultimately creates an energy of physical density—a bodily symptom: sickness, illness, dis-ease. In the case of love, it creates a symptom in the location where expressions of love take place in a person's physical/non-physical energy structure—their heart area: its energy portal, the heart chakra; its associated gland, the thymus; and the related organ, the heart itself. If the root blockage or resistance is not dealt with in the subtler emotional and mental levels, this results in heart disease of one kind or another at the physical level.

The undoing of disease has nothing to do with the outer symptoms; they're only the effects, the signals to be observed and interpreted as guidance to the inner cause. Dealing only with symptoms only covers the message, smothering the guidance that's there for your highest good and learning.

The true and permanent undoing of disease is the result of harmonizing uneasiness; in other words, neutralizing conflicts—*inner* conflicts. This is energy transmutation, or genuine healing; the dissolving of personal energy blocks.

The will and effort to accept, identify, understand, and dissolve one's own damaging resistances, biases, conditioning, preconceptions, conflicts and judgments can be considered one of the most significant self healing, self loving activities and consciousness-raising disciplines that anyone can undertake.

Opening your own channel—your personal physical/non-physical energy system of mind, emotions and body—to a greater flow of spontaneous life force energy is the single most effective and rapid means of enabling the healing process. It requires allowing your life to happen spontaneously with as little resistance on your part as possible.

This brings flexibility, awareness and growth into life, the opposite of rigidity, ignorance and stagnation. It empowers you by introducing opportunities to identify and dissolve your blocks, opportunities in the form of circumstances you may otherwise have avoided. It brings in high frequency energy, of which the main effect is to accentuate by contrast the lower frequency energies such as negativity, limitation and resistance.

It's a little like happily entering a room full of sobbing people—your contrasting high frequency state of joy and happiness can't help but highlight by contrast the misery in the room, and vice versa.

In such ways, opening your channels not only opens you to the rich potential tapestry of life, it also emphasizes your own healing issues arising from your past conditioning that has determined how you respond to present circumstances.

Would your conditioning tell you to feel less happy to match the misery in the room? So that those people would feel less offended by your happiness? Or would it prompt you to help them attain a higher level of joy? Therein lies the issues of courage and integrity, healing and meaningful spiritual growth.

Whenever anyone consciously undertakes to open their channels to higher energies, they immediately begin drawing to themselves a seemingly relentless stream of healing issues and events, each one more intense than the previous. Many find it difficult to muster the inner strength and balance to sustain their exposure to this apparent onslaught.

The only reprieve comes in actually dissolving and healing the disharmony and dis-ease in day-to-day circumstances. Not by 'knowing' it, 'owning' it or 'sharing' it, not by giving it a fancy label or talking about it, but by actually taking the sheer discipline and courage to *do* something about it... namely, to act on your highest truth and sense of self love without compromise, hesitation or exception... relentlessly, in everyday moments and everyday situations with everyday people.

Be unconventional or even shocking if that's what it takes, but don't let that be your motivation. Ensure your heartfelt motivation is always to provide yourself a next step to greater growth, awareness, learning, upliftment, joy. If the resulting effect on others is disturbing then so be it, it was honestly never your intention. They will learn whatever it was they were meant to learn from your truth, not from falsehood of any kind.

Some issues can become so impactful that a person can't believe they had such blocks and resistances to their own unconditional unique expression. Layer upon layer of hurdles and barriers, some subtle and others obvious, are exposed like open wounds which may hurt a little at first but are able to rapidly heal if surrendered up to the transforming life values and conditions fuelled by the new energy and consciousness.

For that reason I consider courageous anyone who chooses to work with direct voice channeling or overt creative expression such as music, art and writing. I similarly view those involved in pure unadulterated spiritual activities, particularly since they must often fly in the face of convention if they're going to act upon what they deeply believe in.

Also commendable are those investing their efforts in ground breaking technological activities such as new inventions, in fresh empowering ideas for future communities and social structures, enlightened governance, holistic and alternative health care, inspired education and sustainable food and fuel technologies and methodologies. These are intended to benefit one and all, not just a select few or the long term detriment of the planet and our species.

Whether or not they're popular, effective, noted or supported, these brave souls are at the cutting edge of the new consciousness. They are the free thinkers, less bound by their own conditioning or by conventional thinking and therefore not needing the approval of the mass mind nor of the status quo attitude.

They're the visionaries who can show how and why humankind might rise out of the mediocrity, injustice, scarcity, conflict, pain and fear that are products of the old belief systems based on limitation, overbearance, control and polarity. They're the ones who can show the way out of victimhood and misery into an Earthly experience of fulfillment through empowerment— mass mastery born of belief systems based on love and creativity and unlimited potentiality; a new world that lies beyond what *appears* to be or what simply suits the popular comfort zone.

These truly courageous warriors of evolutionary spirit and achievement are often considered egocentric, eccentric or downright weird by the mass mentality. They're often even outcast simply because they allow themselves to step beyond their existing boundaries in all sorts of ways, putting their heart on their sleeve and their unique personal truth on the line.

But what's comfortable is not always right and what's right is certainly not always comfortable as was illustrated by such people as Leonardo da Vinci, Jesus, Copernicus, Lao Tzu, Joan of Arc, Galileo, Nikolai Teslar, Mozart, Buddha, Albert Einstein, Princess Diana. They and numerous others have made a real difference to the true progress of human evolution, awareness or empowerment. They consciously chose not to tow the status quo line; not to reinforce the comfortable and comforting falsehoods, illusions and injustices nor support the predominance of human ego and comfort zone compromises.

Whether they have known it or not, such individuals became open channels for the Supreme inspiration that's *available to one and all*. They enable a world of crushing mediocrity, disharmony and misdirection to bathe in the warm light of hope in a higher order of life, and to enjoy increasing manifestations of the Great Dream coming to reality... for everyone.

LIFE SUPPORT SYSTEM

Your physical body is a little like a car. Just as the car contains all the components that the complete automobile needs to serve as transportation, so your body contains the vital elements of your consciousness in a way that allows you to fulfill your purpose by experiencing a physical life.

That being the case, it's your responsibility to take care of it. It houses your vital chassis, the structure and network by which the more subtle, complex, feeling and thinking part of you—your energy field—can be conscious, active and expressive in a physical world.

Upon first encountering and trying to understand this system it can be a little bewildering and difficult to grasp. It can appear as though your energy portals (chakras) are simply ways of energizing different bodily parts and functions. They certainly are that, but they're much more as well.

Your chakras are the means by which you conduct the life force energy from its source into your life, thereby expressing yourself into your reality. Your own life is essentially your individual way of doing just that—experiencing your consciousness in a unique combination of thoughts and beliefs, awareness and perceptions, emotions and words, activities and movements.

As potent energy portals, your chakras also sustain your physical form by maintaining a system which steps down pure life force into arrangements and compositions of energy that your physical body systems can receive and use as sustenance.

This energy system also organizes and vitalizes the material substance of your body so that you can take material form and do things. Your actions are made possible by the natural cooperation of all the energies that interact with your body, creating and sustaining you as a physical human on Earth.

To do so, your chakras are integral with your physical body in a sequence that enables your physical body to be formed and maintained. They manifest as electrical energy, atoms, DNA and RNA, nervous energy through the nervous system, chemicals and hormones, and ultimately the physical energy including glands, organs, cells, fluids, tissues and skeletal structure.

Every form and function that comprises you and your existence is the same fundamental life force energy manifesting in this variety of ways by maintaining myriad vibrational patterns and frequencies. Through this system, the Cosmic Law of Creation (as above, so below) ensures that the frequencies above (non-physical thoughts, beliefs, attitudes and emotions) will determine how the frequencies below (the physical tissues and bodily structure) manifest in form as it steps down through the scales of frequencies.

Over time, this Cosmic Law draws all of our gross physical form and functions into alignment with our more subtle emotional, mental and spiritual ones. That makes your entire body an exact physical model of the beliefs, attitudes, biases and conditioning, that you've upheld to date. As is what you see as your outer reality.

Your state of consciousness and the way you're using it will invariably be reflected to you as your personal experience of life. Put another way, your reality only changes to reflect you, not to please or to displease you.

Your body is your own vehicle for you to fulfill your life purpose. It's your personal responsibility to take care of, maintain, nourish and use it. This is one of your spiritual responsibilities and the basis of karma. Many people believe that karma is God's punishment for something they did wrong; a kind of cosmic accounts ledger of good and bad behavior. But in God's eyes nothing is right or wrong nor good or bad.

The point of view that karma is punishment can be, and frequently is, used to justify otherwise damaging, abusive or unhealthy behavior as much as it's used to deter it. How many times have you heard such comments as "Oh, it must be their karma" or "They must have deserved it" to absolve what was otherwise inexcusable behavior?

In the most objective terms, karma is neither good nor bad—it just boils down to our own self-created experiences. If the experience seems like a 'punishment' then it's self inflicted by the sufferer. After all, it's only able to manifest as a result of them persistently investing the required amount of energy in beliefs and attitudes that are self punishing or disharmonious concerning themselves or their reality. The Law of Karma—cause and effect; the Cosmic Law of Creation. Seen in this light, karma is actually empowering and liberating, not the punishing and controlling force that victim-minded people prefer to see it or use it as to confirm, endorse or excuse their 'poor me' syndrome.

How you sustain your life, express yourself in every conceivable way, and be aware of and create your reality in its rich tapestry of infinite variety and potential, is the product of your own chakra system. In this way, the portals of light that are your chakras are more than simply a way of forming and sustaing your body.

Figure 3

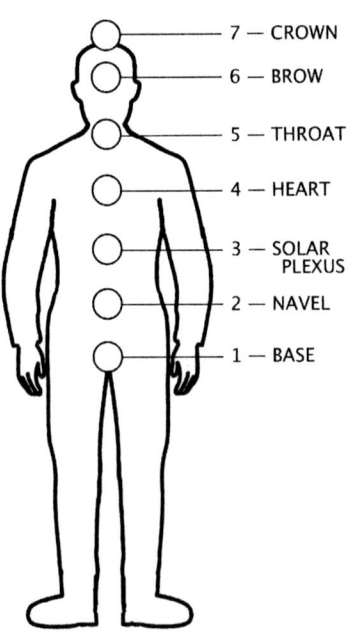

7 — CROWN

6 — BROW

5 — THROAT

4 — HEART

3 — SOLAR PLEXUS

2 — NAVEL

1 — BASE

PORTALS OF LIGHT

Each of the seven major chakras in your body enables you to express and sense a different attribute of life. They're the ways that you can be aware of life and the ways you can effect the type of person that you're being within your life—your personal traits and idiosyncrasies. This system doesn't define qualities as good or bad, it just provides the means to experience all life.

In terms of frequency, or rate of vibration, the higher the chakra in your body (e.g. crown), the higher in consciousness are its attributes; the lower the chakra (e.g. base) the lower the consciousness it expresses. This mirrors other phenomena in our outer world which are also attributed to the chakras, most notably the various hues of color and tones of sound.

The spectrum spans from red and the sound tone C, which are attributed to the base chakra, rising through the scales to violet and the sound tone B relating to the crown chakra. *(Figure 3.)* Just as the basic seven notes in the musical scale span one octave of sounds that we can hear, so do our seven basic chakras span one octave of our human existence (the embodied, physical, material level of life). In turn each of the seven major chakras spans one sector or type of experience we may have within our physical life, examples being experiences of thought or of touch, of sight or emotion.

Colors and musical notes are frequencies in the spectrum of electromagnetic energy as described by the current field of science. You'll relate to and experience them in day-to-day life through sight and hearing.

The only difference is that the octaves of sound and light at the chakra level of your energy system are far above levels that normal human senses can detect—people can neither hear a dog whistle nor the inner pulse of the Earth (called the Schumann Resonance). Neither can they see ultraviolet or infrared light. Those frequencies of energy are outside the range of normal human senses. We can only detect, measure and observe them by employing specialized instruments which serve as an interface between us and the myriad other frequency levels of energy in our world.

Each chakra, with its associated color and sound, works within boundaries of frequencies. Outside its boundaries are adjacent chakras with their own related colors and sounds. *(Figure 4.)* Together they form a continuous, seamless scale of frequencies.

Within its own boundaries, each chakra creates an infinitely subtle and variable scale of frequencies encapsulating its particular consciousness scale or category such as mental energy, or emotional energy.

If its category is say, the mental energy of life, then absolutely all variations of the thinking side of life are included—thoughts can be fleeting or lingering, loving or fearful, complimentary or contradictory, confused or clear, beneficial or evil, destructive or constructive, harmonious or conflicting, expansive or restrictive, and so on.

The more fearful, restrictive or rigid the characteristic (for example, a controlling or dominating attitude), the lower is the consciousness being expressed and the lower the frequency at which the chakra is functioning. The more allowing and flexible (such as a tolerant, non-confrontational or flexible attitude), the higher is the consciousness and higher the frequency.

Also, there comes a stage where each chakra blends into—and thereby becomes—adjacent chakras. In the case of thought energy, at its lower boundary it blends into emotion and into insight at its upper limit. Having reached those stages, the energy corresponds to other chakras and no longer comes under the jurisdiction of the thinking process. This is why emotion and intuition make little or no sense to the rational mind.

Likewise, in the sense of tone, the chakra pertaining

Figure 4

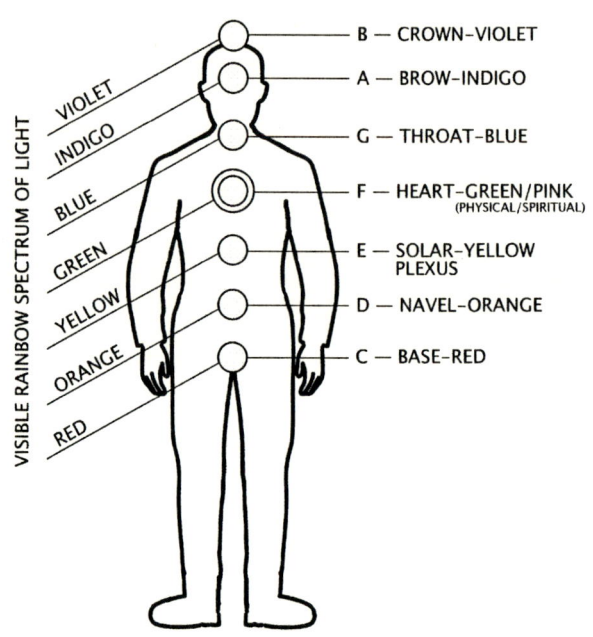

VISIBLE RAINBOW SPECTRUM OF LIGHT

VIOLET
INDIGO
BLUE
GREEN
YELLOW
ORANGE
RED

B — CROWN-VIOLET

A — BROW-INDIGO

G — THROAT-BLUE

F — HEART-GREEN/PINK
(PHYSICAL/SPIRITUAL)

E — SOLAR-YELLOW
PLEXUS

D — NAVEL-ORANGE

C — BASE-RED

to the spectrum of sound tone E, for example, has infinitely subtle variations before it becomes D sharp at its lower boundary and F at its upper.

Within their own boundaries, colors also display infinite variation as witnessed in the smooth blending of the spectrum in a rainbow. Outside its own boundaries, each color becomes another color, such as yellow turning into orange at the low end of its scale and into green at the high end.

Similarly, your expression of consciousness through your chakras is infinitely subtle. Emotion becomes physical (form and action) at its low boundary and mental (thought and attitude) past its highest limit. It remains, however, all exactly the same fundamental energy, just existing at a different frequency. You'd recognize its analogy in water, which is still the same water irrespective of whether it takes the form of ice, liquid or steam.

The combination of your seven main chakras, each with its own infinite potential, enables you to enjoy infinitely subtle variation in the ways you experience life and express yourself. This ensures your uniqueness as a vital individual spark of the one life force, determined constantly by your own free will in how you choose to use it; by your perceptions and beliefs and how you choose to apply them in your life.

PRACTICALITIES
OF THE CHAKRAS

I describe human chakras in terms of their being higher or lower. Besides reflecting their position in the human body when standing upright, those terms also reflect each chakra's energy frequency relative to the others. It also delineates its functions and expressions in terms of high or low consciousness.

Though the chakras are all fully interactive, I also find it helpful to differentiate the lower three chakras from the higher ones. This helps to clarify the understanding of the human physical world experience (the lower three chakras) and the human spiritual world experience (the higher chakras). *(Figure 4.)*

Representing the categories of human consciousness, the chakras are the way we're conscious of who we are and of being alive.

In practical terms, the lower the frequency, the more a chakra displays through our life the attributes of low consciousness: fear, control, resistance, conditionality, conflict, judgment, pain, scarcity, hardship and disease.

The higher the frequency, the greater our expression of the qualities of higher levels of consciousness: love, allowance, peace, harmony, unconditionality, opportunity, joy, abundance and wellbeing. Therefore love, abundance, wellbeing and peace equate with a higher pitch sound and higher frequency color than do fear, scarcity, disease and disharmony. Think for a moment about sound: a series of notes in an ascending scale seem more pleasing, uplifting and positive than those in a descending series.

Figure 5

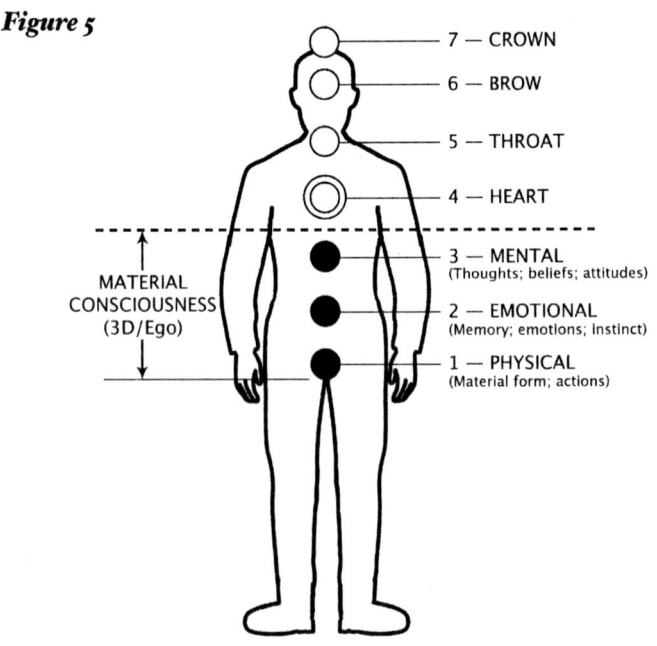

7 — CROWN

6 — BROW

5 — THROAT

4 — HEART

3 — MENTAL
(Thoughts; beliefs; attitudes)

2 — EMOTIONAL
(Memory; emotions; instinct)

1 — PHYSICAL
(Material form; actions)

MATERIAL
CONSCIOUSNESS
(3D/Ego)

THE LOWER CHAKRAS

As humans we've been living in three dimensional consciousness, or 3D as it's often called. This means we've had only three tools at our disposal with which to experience life and to interact with and understand our world. We've been limited to living only three aspects of our true unlimited potential.

How exactly this situation has come about is explained fully in my book *From Atoms to Angels*. Briefly, it's by our own choosing and this self limitation is the origin of our present conflict-saturated reality and our fear- and polarity-based lives. By persisting in believing we're separate, the ego also believes that, in order to survive and feel worthy or valuable, it must make itself better, more and right for fear of being bad, less or wrong. It tries to control life to that end, only to find itself trapped in a complicated net of conflict, struggle, disallowance and judgment as a result.

The three dimensions to which we find ourselves and our lives limited—physical, emotional and mental—function through the three lower chakras. (*Figure 5.*) We've spent vast amounts of evolutionary time becoming conditioned to working with only these few facets of an otherwise unlimited array of consciousness equipment.

The result is that, other than these three, nothing *seems* to make sense; nothing else *seems* real. We've evolved to believe that there is no real way to experience, live, understand or define life other than in physical, emotional and mental terms. Fortunately, that's only our belief, not the truth of the matter. These three only facilitate the lowest three dimensions of awareness, the lowest frequency octaves of energy that we can utilize in life.

The First Chakra

On the scale of human consciousness, the lowest band of frequencies are associated with the base chakra and manifest as survival instinct; fight or flight.

This chakra becomes hyperactive when a person believes they're in life threatening circumstances where they must choose quickly how they'll stay alive; will they run away to fight another day or stay and fight the foe now? Having identified a situation as life threatening in some way, the person's thoughts and beliefs about it activate an instantaneous message system within. The base chakra wants to do something about it. Impressions of the threat are sent to the brain where they're evaluated against existing knowledge and understandings. Which course of action seems to give a better chance of surviving the day? Electrical and nervous impulses engage and supply of the hormone adrenaline enables the person's body to respond quickly.

In this way, the base chakra functions in conjunction with the adrenal glands, but also in association with the spinal column, kidneys and reproduction and evacuation systems. It's very intense and 'physical' energy, as it drives our most basic instinct—keep on living; keep on experiencing life; preserve the physical body.

Resonating principally to the color red, the base

chakra is located at the perineum, between the legs near the base of the spine. Arousing survival instinct or the need to take physical action stimulates this chakra, drawing energy to it from and through the body's overall energy system. If fear for survival calls for extreme action, excess energy will be directed to the base chakra and can cause quite dramatic physical effects.

In a simple and common form, this can be seen when someone goes 'weak at the knees' or becomes paralyzed when frightened, unable to move at all. Such effects are created when a massive amount of energy is suddenly directed in the instant away from their general overall being and into the specific notion of the fear itself.

I have a friend in New Zealand who experienced remarkable effects of this 'physical' energy. He is admittedly a very well built, strong man but he even surprised himself when he encountered a situation where his young son became trapped under the front of his van. His spontaneous unthinking response to the sudden and dreadful circumstance was to lift the van off his son—which he did, remarkably, while bystanders dragged the boy free.

He and everyone present were absolutely astounded at what he'd done, knowing that in normal circumstances he could never have managed to lift the front of the van, particularly considering the weight of its engine. But his base chakra had burst into full power in the situation of life and death, enabling such an extraordinary physical action to be taken. If he'd directed mental energy into the situation instead, thinking rationally according to his existing beliefs about himself, he would've undoubtedly convinced himself that he couldn't have lifted the van and the result would have been fatal. But instead, that mental energy was mobilized into emotional energy—his feelings for his son—and then physical energy, supercharging his physical form with every iota of his life force to achieve a superhuman act of physical strength. His son was not fatally injured.

All of this happens in a fraction of a second where time doesn't allow for decisions and responses to be rational or conscious. They become unconscious, instinctive. In such circumstances it's largely our subconscious self with all its pre-conditioning, that actually controls how our conscious physical self behaves.

We find simple instances of this in everyday life, situations where most people find no problem yet someone suddenly behaves irrationally or out of character. Being afraid to scale a stairway or stand near a cliff edge or being frightened to travel in a speeding car are examples. The fear of heights, enclosed spaces or wide open spaces, flying, swimming, public speaking and other phobias and anxieties are all typical.

Such fears and resistances are most often caused by previous experiences—even childhood or past life— which are brought up for healing by the unique nature of the moment the person is experiencing in the Now.

The effects of conditioning have been buried very deep below the conscious surface, having been repeatedly pushed so far back into the inner dungeons of avoidance and denial that it can take extremely intense circumstances to dislodge them and bring them to the surface again for healing (which they must do if future physical disease is to be avoided). This also illustrates why courageously facing our fears and dealing with extreme or desperate situations in a way that upholds our innermost truth enables us to extend beyond our existing boundaries and grow.

Nobody is immune to this phenomenon; there is always some instance where a person behaves as they would not normally have done, had there been more time or less pressure placed upon them, or maybe if the circumstances or their past had been just a little different.

An interesting example is the number of people who become involved in death defying pursuits or dangerous sports. They seem to crave overcoming or cheating the threat of death. Not surprising in light of today's lifestyles, increasingly insured against risk and sterilized of uncertainty and even of personal responsibility.

In ages past such pursuits wouldn't have crossed people's minds simply because of the threatening nature of daily life itself; every day was a death defying act of survival! The underlying purpose though is to keep the base chakra active and get the 'rush' of the adrenaline flow so that the body can know it's alive. The energy of raw survival, which is very stimulating and even addictive, reminds them that they're mortal. It generally contrasts a daily lifestyle which they find unstimulating, one in which everything has been put through the status quo blanding machine to the extent that they actually no longer *feel* alive.

This is one of the reasons why living in the moment, living spontaneously, is so healing. It's reveling in the unpredictability of life rather than fearing it. This spontaneous type of 'living dangerously' brings to the surface more of the real issues that are deep in the unconscious conditioning where they're lowering the person's vibration and threatening or causing disease mentally, emotionally or physically.

The intensity that's felt through surrendering to the Now experience is, in itself, a vital healing opportunity. It makes conscious what was unconscious by highlighting the hidden conditioning that usually motivates a person to behave involuntarily or irrationally in an effort to avoid, intellectualize, deny or plain lie to themselves to protect the ego and the self limiting boundaries of its comfort zone.

In instances where a person's rational mind is still able to control the body's actions, it most often does so to the detriment of their own healing and their long term physical, emotional and mental wellbeing.

In the case of the man lifting the van, the consequences of engaging the rational mind would have been fatal. Instead, though, he found out something empowering about himself that he would previously have denied possible.

Such a new self image irrevocably alters people's beliefs and attitudes towards themselves and others, not to mention towards life itself. It expands their consciousness beyond its previous constraints.

Spontaneity—unthinking, unconditioned, immediate response to the deep and instantaneous inner urges in any moment—facilitates healing on an everyday level in everyday lives. But, though it's the center where life force becomes physical, the base chakra is not the sole provider of such healing potential when you open to life.

In similar fashion to the base chakra, each of the other chakras is an avenue to express your awareness and beliefs about life and yourself.

If you have resistances, controls, conditional or limiting beliefs of any kind whatsoever, whether you judge them to be right, justifiable, proper, descent or not, then you'll be congesting the flow of life force through your energy field and depleting your health and energy on all levels. The energy lowers its vibration more and more every time you yield to one of those fear influences in your mind, emotions or actions until eventually it manifests as physical dis-ease in the glands and/or organs which are inextricably linked to the corresponding chakra.

The Second Chakra

Located near the navel, the second chakra's relative color is orange; its sound is note D. It's a hot spot of human nature since it determines how you relate to your world. It employs emotions, conscious and subconscious memory, and past conditioning.

The second chakra is mobilized in circumstances where emotional energy springs forth, especially in sexuality and in all relationships with other people, be they lovers, family, friends, associates, opponents, colleagues or enemies, whether close or distant.

Guilt and confidence are very strong influences in this area since they're your past conditioning, biases and, particularly, judgments being projected onto your present experiences. Emotional attachments to people, ideas, beliefs, experiences and any need or desire to have things the way you insist they be or judge to be good or right, all apply as well.

Censorship of nudity would be a case in point. Many people have been taught to believe that the naked human body is not a decent thing and so must always remain covered. This is typical of the developed or (so called) civilized world. It's quite likely the result simply of some influential individual having been embarrassed about their own body so covering it up and convincing other easily influenced people to do the same until eventually it became accepted on a mass level. But there are also races, religions, civilizations and communities who believe just as strongly that the human body is as natural as flowers, animals, birds or trees and see nothing distasteful or unwholesome at all in it being exposed. In fact some openly accentuate body parts that they're proud of but which others hide away under shame or fear of ridicule. So if there was indeed a right and wrong, then who is right and who is wrong? Both beliefs are based on equally valid previous attitudes handed down through generations and treated with equal sincerity, faith and commitment.

Neither is right nor wrong, good nor bad; they're just different.

This issue reminds me of the story of the King's New Clothes—who is the authority in your life? You or someone else? Who calls the shots?

Who else can possibly know what's best for you and your highest good? What's right is not always popular and what's popular is not always right. Do you just adhere to the mass preferences, whether they're ideal or not, or do you have the confidence to act upon a mind of your own, guided by what's deeply true to you personally, taking responsibility for educating and maintaining that inner truth in a healthy and vital state? Self confidence is a powerful component of the second chakra's energies.

Two people facing the same task may have opposite beliefs, one believing they can, the other believing they can't. And both are correct! But only insofar as they have each learned and accepted their respective opposing beliefs. And their experience will ultimately pan out to prove it, every move and decision they make being molded by memories buried deep in the cells of their body.

Sensations that arise in relation to your outer circumstances—flushes of embarrassment, anger, shame, guilt and the like—are all the effects of cellular memory. The cells have stored the emotional effects of past experiences and responses that have seemed real and meaningful at some time to the individual. Those effects are stored in deep memory as pure intangible energy locked within the actual cells and tissues of the body.

The person's consciousness recognizes certain

circumstances by their characteristics. When the situations arise, the body is prompted to respond in recognition by mobilizing the stored energy as a reference point for action. Within the tissues of the body, one then feels the energy in motion—*e-motion*, in the form of hot flushes, shaking, tears, perspiration and the like.

The emotions you feel in life are actually the effects of the stored energy being triggered and mobilized into the tissues. They influence you to act again—to *re-act*—the way you did in the circumstances when those energies were originally stored in the distant past.

For that reason, even in new and different experiences your reactions can be intense and seem irrational and unrelated to the actual attributes of the circumstances you've encountered. It may feel overwhelmingly strong and correct yet make absolutely no sense at all. This can be to the detriment of any benefit a new experience might offer. Take for example a tough, city-wise woman I knew in America who fainted when her boyfriend proposed to her!

The ego, obsessed by its physical-body-based interpretation of all that is, nevertheless persists in using the stored energies of the past to stop you upsetting its familiar comfort zone; to stop you from growing into newness through the adventure of life.

All emotion is the energy of long term memory becoming mobilized in the body's tissues, aroused by circumstances that prompt that particular recall. They're not good or bad, right or wrong, just habit. Nothing more, nothing less.

Problems arise only when the emotional person tries to hide or suppress the emotion in the belief that there is something 'wrong' with them because it doesn't feel 'right'. That just pushes the energy inwards once again, feeding it, making it even stronger and enabling reactions to be even more intense and irrational next time.

Not until the ill-at-ease energy (disease) is dissolved from static form (physical) into fluid form (emotional) can it be recognized (felt) and then corrected (healed). That is to say, if you don't feel it, you can't heal it—you'll only think you've healed it.

If you harbor resistances, fears, conditionality, judgment, disallowance, controlling tendencies or emotional attachments of any kind in the area of sexual and relationship experiences in your life, then you're congesting the energy in your second chakra. Unless released, such attitudes and beliefs will inevitably become disease in your reproductive system as well as in your emotional subconscious memory storehouse—your abdomen area: stomach, intestines, colon, reproductive, urinary and digestive systems and your spleen, all of which are associated with and linked to your second chakra.

Dissolving and releasing potential dis-ease related to the second chakra requires that you go about dissolving all of your judgments, conditionality, controls and disallowance concerning the way relationships (yours and others') are. It also requires letting go of the way you believe things 'should' be.

Let go of what you can't have without controlling

it or setting conditions in some way. Stop trying to force or coerce others into meeting your needs or living up to your image or expectations of them. Stop judging others to be right or wrong, good or bad and instead just let them be themselves, whether you agree with or approve of them or not. Begin stepping past your lack of self confidence whenever it arises. Identify when you're feeling guilty and reconsider your attitudes, beliefs and thoughts in any way that'll render the guilt unnecessary or obsolete. It doesn't matter what you choose to think, no matter how outrageous or unconventional or shocking in terms of yours or anyone else's habits of believing, it will definitely be closer to Supreme Truth by mere virtue of its contradicting the need to feel guilty.

Everyone faces circumstances that trigger strong sensations of their energy of memory and conditioning flowing through their tissues as e-motion. Therefore any strong feeling is a healing opportunity; an opportunity to both dissolve existing disease in your body as well as potential disease from manifesting in the future. Again: if you can't feel it you can't heal it.

By allowing yourself to experience the circumstances and feel the associated emotional energies instead of resisting, controlling or suppressing them, you'll enable your congested energies to become accessible to the healing process. You'll know when they are accessible because you'll be feeling the emotions!

Whilst feeling emotions—and only whilst actually feeling them in their full intensity—you have the opportunity to dissolve potential disease from your tissues and cells once and for all, if you're willing. You can do so simply by asking yourself *"What do I need to alter* inside me *in order to feel completely at peace with this situation? What ideas or beliefs or needs or judgments must I change* within me *to be in a balanced and tolerant state?"*

Do you need to begin believing that you are not weak or that you are allowed to believe certain things? Do you need to start thinking that it's okay for someone else to have different views or attitudes to yours? Do you need to stop trying to make people agree with you or believe you? Do you need to accept and relish differences or uniqueness instead of finding it challenging? Is it time you to give up the belief that you need to satisfy others expectations of you? Are you being inflexible or fighting and prolonging conflict just to prove a point... or to win... or to feel right? Is it time to relinquish a need to strive to be accepted or recognized or approved of? What do you truly need to address inside yourself in order to be at peace?

Be brutally honest with yourself in establishing the issue or issues because they're the cornerstone of dis-ease. The more honest and accurate you are in this process, the more immediate and effective will be your healing. You do not need to accept what you don't agree with or what doesn't feel true to you, but you do need to embrace an open state of mind that'll allow it all to exist in the world, with or without your resistance to it or approval of it.

Next, act accordingly. Having established what needs to be changed within, make the changes...

within... there and then. Now. Right now whilst in the feelings. That'll eliminate the cause of disease. Just removing symptoms does nothing but feel better for now; it only delays a more intense onset later. Removing the actual cause, on the other hand, is the only true sustainable cure for any disease.

Finally, begin applying the same process to all circumstances in your life, starting with the ones that upset you the most. It may require repeated exposure and relentless self discipline, courage and inner strength, but only you can do it.

That makes just three steps to lasting self health and spiritual growth:

Step One: Feel experiences instead of avoiding them.

Step Two: Ask yourself what you'd need to change *inside yourself* in order to be at peace with what is, allowing it to be and not resisting it.

Step Three: Make those changes inside.

Eventually, by taking true spiritual responsibility for yourself and your life this way, your behavior will no longer be controlled by conditioning because the stored energies will have become exhausted. Instead you'll feel at peace with life and see all things through more enlightened, detached eyes.

Also, in your calmness you'll be able to evaluate everything according to your own inner truth and highest good, rather than just by unconscious reactions based on habitual judgment and self limiting, self imposed biases. Your own Inner Truth will become your authority at all times instead of the second hand, worn out, faded opinions of the mass mentality and self appointed authorities intent on influencing your every move to meet their own diseased expectations and biases.

Some of the conditioning you'll encounter in this process can be so habitual or extremely subtle that you'll not realize you're doing it or that you're reacting as you are. Therefore another spiritual discipline is imperative in order to become self aware—constant self analysis of all attitudes and actions. An enormous helping of self honesty is also vital.

Love and respect yourself enough to be open, forthright, honest and above all objective toward yourself and your attitudes and actions in every single moment. Then apply that objectivity to others as well, not to change them but to discern what's useful to your own self wisdom and self loving activities and what's not.

The Third Chakra

The next higher chakra in the scale is the third, the highest of the lower three. Situated at the solar plexus, its color is yellow; note E. It's all about mental energy—thoughts, learning, beliefs, analysis, intellect, rationality, knowledge and attitude.

Since, in the flow of creation into our dense realm and in alignment with immutable Cosmic Law of 'as above, so below,' thought energy precedes emotional and physical forms of energy, then it stands to reason that the solar plexus and third chakra is the creative center of our 3D lives and world.

Most people think of creativity in terms of art, music, literature or inventions or similar overt examples of the creative force. But *everyone* is creative. I refer to everyone's irrefutable and irrevocable ability to create their own life's circumstances by first allowing original thought to occur (that is, thinking for themselves instead of just thinking what they're told or convinced to think) and then focusing their thought energy on the thought forms (ideas and beliefs) that they find most fulfilling, inspiring and exhilarating. This, as opposed to thinking only in line with the mass mentality, bending and compromising to fit in regardless of whether it paints a pleasant and supportive or an unpleasant and discouraging picture of life.

A dis-eased solar plexus chakra will first become evident in non-physical symptoms such as worry, anger and expectation or fearful, rigid and controlling attitudes such as secrecy and manipulation. Also in tendencies to be judgmental, inflexible and dogmatic in thinking and beliefs and even in excessive or rigid planning for the future. But as is the case with all levels of consciousness, mental energy must and will eventually become physical experience.

Consistent patterns of mental energy (attitudes, thoughts and beliefs) will create exact models in physical form, faster and more vividly according to how faithfully they're sustained. Consistent disharmonious (dis-eased) thoughts will create a dis-eased reality; consistent attitudes of harmony will create harmonious conditions equally well and faithfully. Whether the mental patterns are beneficial or damaging, positive or negative is incidental. A negative mentality will inevitably create a negative reality and a positive mentality, a positive reality. Simple... and infallible.

Disharmony and conflict in the mental levels of consciousness will eventually produce physical symptoms of the dis-ease correspondingly in the pancreas, liver, gall bladder and diaphragm area. They become eliminated simply through converting to high frequency mental energy—allowing, embracing and exploring your own and others' original thinking. Original thought is creative thought—the thoughts whose origin is within you. Original thought is one thing of which everyone is capable and which nobody can stop you using unless you so choose.

High frequency mental energy is not afraid of its uniqueness nor of any other, instead relishing expressions of flexible thinking, unbounded perspectives, originality, openness to learn and develop and grow.

Rather than adhering to or reinforcing boundaries, high mental consciousness challenges them, expressing unbounded creativity and adventurous, joyous exploration of possibility and the yet unknown. At the same time it applies rational structure to bring inspired, imaginative, inventive ideas into actual reality in all areas of life, thereby assisting the flow of Creation instead of blocking it.

When you're ready to embrace your higher consciousness, you'll find that the key is to allow your mental energy to evolve through honest and diligent assessment and reconstruction of your attitudes and beliefs, with the consistent intention to bring them into alignment with Cosmic Law. Thus, you gift yourself the ultimate creative opportunity—deliberately creating the life you choose in every moment, in every detail.

Only through opening your mind to an evolutionary quantum leap into the unfamiliar higher levels of your consciousness will your mind become the active creative force instead of a passive creative source.

THE HEART
OF THE MATTER

We have another four chakras integral with our physical body. We can choose to make use of these as well if we wish, along with their specific attributes, just as we do the lower ones.

However, due to our ego's persistent preoccupation with the lower three, the upper chakras have largely been ignored. After all, having three tools that seem useful, practical and real, everything else became relegated to the 'not real' category. It attracted the term *spiritual*, a label which automatically branded such matters impractical, idealistic, unrealistic or even useless. Of course rational, realistic human beings learned not to waste their time entertaining such far fetched ethereal issues...

The only exceptions are the relatively few people who bothered to learn about and express their higher consciousness, love and creativity, usually through purely spiritual teachings and practices.

By understanding, cultivating and applying the attributes of their higher chakras in real life, such people reached through the barrier that had separated them from higher consciousness and higher knowing. Due to their viewpoint on life being unhindered by the common consciousness of their time, such people often suffered ridicule, incarceration, excommunication, punishment, exile, torture or even death for their unconventional, nonconformist principles.

Nonetheless, detached from the shackles of limited understanding and limiting beliefs about themselves and their world, and by honoring and expressing their expanded view of life through their teachings and activities, they eventually became revered as spiritual masters and leaders, gurus or messiahs, even geniuses. Ironically, they became exalted often by the very people who'd earlier decried their principles so vehemently.

Yet all the while they were just surrendering to what was outside their own preconceptions and conditioning; beyond their accepted comfort zone and their limitations. They were taking responsibility for opening to life and embracing the new potential that was revealed to them through their embracing the planes of higher consciousness—by the agency of their higher chakras.

What has happened to the majority of humankind however is that this 3D reality of ours has congealed into something that seems so solid that it appears to be the only possible way to live. And indeed it is, at least for anyone who chooses to live by only their lower three chakras—by only the mental, emotional and physical qualities of life.

When we transcend the veil between our lower and higher consciousness, though, our perception expands past its previous threshold and reaches our heart chakra and beyond. This exposes us to a whole new additional spectrum of life potential and experience, one that's founded in higher consciousness.

This new life begins to integrate unconditional

love along with faith in oneself and trust in the cosmically perfect natural flow of creation. It also induces the courage to bathe in that flow with as little resistance as possible. These qualities blossom through the heart chakra—note F. *(Figure 6.)*

Figure 6

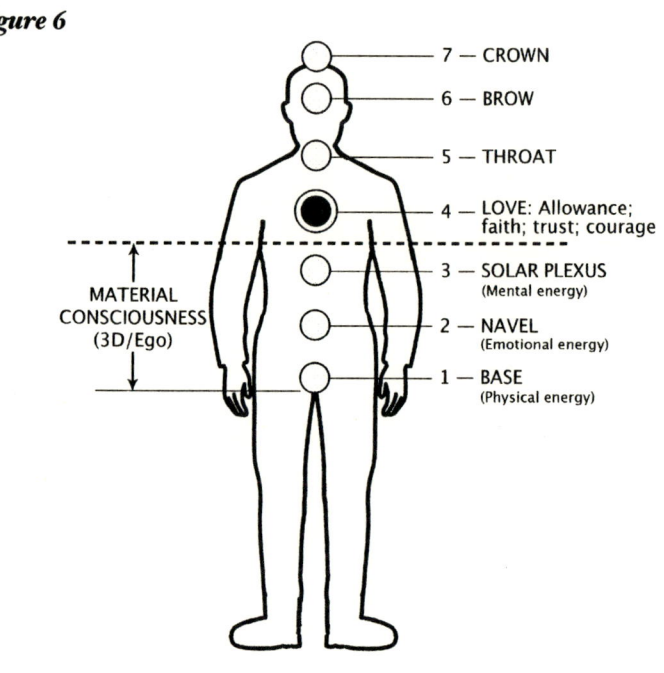

7 — CROWN

6 — BROW

5 — THROAT

4 — LOVE: Allowance; faith; trust; courage

3 — SOLAR PLEXUS (Mental energy)

2 — NAVEL (Emotional energy)

1 — BASE (Physical energy)

MATERIAL CONSCIOUSNESS (3D/Ego)

Like the other chakras of the body, the heart chakra supports a physical organ as well as a gland. In the case of the heart center, a distinction is made between the heart organ (resonating to the color green) which pumps blood, and the heart gland, the thymus (resonating to pink) which processes the deep feelings and sensitivities experienced when a person begins to integrate unconditional love, trust, faith and courage into their life.

With the monumental shift that's now happening in humankind's consciousness, the heart chakra is awakening. It's enabling humankind to move into a new age of evolution where all life is becoming based on unconditional love (allowance, peace, harmony, balance and equality) instead of fear (control, conflict, competition and hierarchy).

With seven major chakras in the physical body, the lower three are often thought of as pertaining to the physical world and the top three to the spiritual world. The heart chakra in the center and its attributes of love, courage and faith are considered the crucial link between the physical self and the spiritual self, or the ego and the soul. The connection provided by this portal presents us the opportunity to evolve into, live and benefit from higher states of consciousness.

Upon activation of the heart chakra, the present limited and limiting reality can do nothing but dissolve in the face of higher frequencies of energy like ice dissolving in the presence of steam. The warmth of humankind's own love and higher self realization—awareness of its fundamental spiritual nature, cosmic essence and profound potency opens a pathway of higher evolution; a process of deep and far reaching change on all levels.

The transformation begins by highlighting the conflicts that appear when the new vibrations of unconditional allowance mix with the old paradigm of judgment, rigidity and control. These conflicts raise myriad issues of deep conditioning, issues that for many people have become very comfortable like an old favorite pair of shoes.

But by the same token, these comfortable patterns have crippled any chance of reaching true fulfillment. Some people even find themselves holding on vehemently to their self limiting conditioning. When their heart is not open, they can't seem to find the courage within themselves to trust what the flow of creation might bring to replace the limitation and dissatisfaction that's smothering their lives. Their trusted comfort zone has become no more than the devil they know. Little do they realize that if they were to choose the way of the heart's peace, faith and allowance, the substitute would be self power and unquestionable sovereignty over every moment, every circumstance and every experience of their life.

I know from my years in Hong Kong that it can be a daunting prospect surrendering to far reaching change in your life, not to mention accepting your own responsibility for wielding the unlimited power that's inherent in such sovereignty. After all, it's initially in absolute conflict with the entire meaning of life as it has been.

How can you believe and find solace in the old axiom that life 'happens to you' or 'does things to you' whilst at the same time realize that you are sovereign creator of it? How could this be? Releasing the conflict, albeit ideological, requires reconciling the polar opposites by letting go of one belief or the other. Their conflict within you disturbs your fundamental grip on life itself.

You can however choose which belief suits you and what you want out of life. Opening the heart by clearing the heart chakra, or heart consciousness, of past conditioning exposes us to feelings that we may not remember ever having before, which is why it also engenders the attributes of courage (to face those feelings) and faith (in them being beneficial to your growth), both of which are functions of trust. Kahlil Gibran is quoted as saying "Doubt is a pain too lonely to know that faith is its twin brother."

Trust is a major attribute of the heart chakra. Trust is an appreciation of things yet unseen, based on the assumption that creation is a loving and supportive force only. It's a sign that we accept our connectedness with all of creation and hold a deep unshakable understanding that all of life occurs by the perfect workings of natural Cosmic Law, albeit imperfectly perceived by humankind.

Such understanding instills the courage and self love to surrender to the natural flow of life—to delight in life and all its unpredictable adventure instead of resisting or fearing it.

By surrendering to the gifts that each moment holds instead of judging or avoiding them, we're acknowledging the Supreme perfection of the natural uninhibited flow of creation through our own channels from our infinitely wise and loving Higher Self. We're also releasing fear and control, strengthening the understanding that we're absolutely safe in our adventure through life since our own Higher Self will guide us only to the perfect experiences through which our unlimited potential can unfold... if we should stop, relax and listen to it.

That personal shift from fear to love brings its joys and surprises and its healing opportunities, as well as its inevitable conflicts with existing self limiting habits.

Having any resistance to, or inner conflict with, the principle of giving and receiving unconditional love—unconditional allowance—of self or others is detrimental to the health of the heart chakra as well as the thymus gland and heart organ that are inextricably dependent upon it.

Typical is the faulty belief that giving is better than receiving. Like many people, I learned that same belief as a child and accepted it. But that doesn't make it correct. I've since learned that it teaches an unwillingness to receive in all areas of life. It teaches rejection, self punishment, guilt and imbalance, which are all in conflict with the fundamental forces and building blocks of the cosmos—variety, harmony and balance. Conflict with or resistance to the natural way of the cosmos will inevitably result in disease.

Any conflict with the heart's natural attribute of trust, particularly self trust, will cause diseased heart energy. A typical example of the trust conflict is doubting your own Inner Truth—doubting that, if you boldly do what's most deeply true and important to you, then it's automatically going to be for the highest good of everyone involved in the experience or touched by it. Never doubt that.

In place of the Cosmic Law of "Follow your heart at all costs, and all will be in Cosmic Perfection" humanity has instead been bombarded with man made messages of social servitude: Don't trust yourself, trust the status quo. Don't be unique, be conformist. Don't believe in yourself, believe what you're told. Don't be different, be like others. Don't be creative, be conservative. Don't be confident, be conciliatory. Don't reject anything, accept what you're given. Don't venture outside the walls, stay within the known boundaries.

Detachment is the only real cure to this mediocrity epidemic that's swept our species. The powerless homogeny line that we've diligently towed since time immemorial is akin to an umbilical cord—though it served a purpose, it's not actually healthy to stay connected to it. When you're detached it doesn't mean that you don't care or don't love. It also doesn't mean that you're uninvolved in situations that matter nor that you're without compassion concerning other people and their circumstances. It doesn't mean you lose anything or anyone nor that you cut things out of your life.

Genuine detachment is inward, not outward. It's a high consciousness state that means no outside conditions or influences decide what you do or think or how you behave, ONLY your own Inner Voice does. This true detachment is a sign that the heart's energy has been truly activated and is being integrated into daily life. Only by detachment can you remain present and involved, loving and sensitive but always in *your* deepest truth and trusting its appropriateness implicitly. Only then can you be a channel for Divine Will and the Highest Good, rather than for the will of the mass mindset of fear, limitation and control.

There's a common example of the self trust issue which plagues society and wellbeing the world over. If you're like me and many others who were taught (mistakenly, I might add) that it's bad to make waves or upset others, you'll especially relate to this common example. Think of how often you compromise what you say or do in order to avoid disturbing the peace, upsetting someone else or conflicting with some popular attitude. This may seem an insignificant issue, but every time you do it you're allowing yourself to be controlled by the fearful influence of self doubt rather than the loving influence of self trust.

I'm certainly not encouraging you to set out with the *intention* to upset others. That'd be as self destructive as suppressing your truth. But if you do compromise a deep truth in yourself, whether your compromise is momentary or prolonged, important to you at the time or not, it's contributing to disease in your heart energy, thymus gland and heart itself. Remain as detached as possible at all times in all circumstances without exception.

The only way to heal or overcome the disease is to

begin to trust implicitly that whatever is most deeply important and true to you in your heart of hearts will bring exactly what's for your highest good and healing. Trust also that whatever supports your own highest good will naturally be for the highest good and healing of everyone else as well. And then act on it, without compromise or hesitation, to the best of your ability. Whether it seems to you or to others that the circumstances are not good or right, it's only the inferior human consciousness of fear and judgment trying to override Higher Will with the self interested little will of egos.

Human judgment can't alter the fact that such actions are for everyone's highest good by mere virtue of their being guided by Higher Intelligence, heart inspired. And so they are, simply because the source of inspiration and motivation for your actions has not been your thinking process, which is so inclined to be clouded by conditioning and habit, but by your deeper urges—your Inner Voice which speaks to you through your heart energy.

Your heart energy is the only way you can convey the Will of the Supreme Intelligence in your life. Your heart center is where Divine Will speaks to you. Its communication is seldom in words or thoughts simply because it would too easy for your mind to distort and interfere using your personal biases. Its exquisite language is most often deep impulses and yearnings; a sense of what's deeply important to you. If anyone is upset as a result, and you can genuinely promise that upset was not the motivation or intention of your action, just a result, then rest assured that it is the natural healing power of your truth emitting through you. Truth can only heal, never harm. Non-truths invariably cause damage and disease.

I'm frequently asked to help people with relationship conflicts. They're increasingly common the world over irrespective of race, creed, religion, culture or socioeconomic standing. I've discovered a common thread in the repair of disharmonious relationships. It goes like this: Relationships are rich environments for learning and healing. The more intimate your relationship, the more intimately and deeply you learn about *yourself*... and heal, if you so choose. The perfect relationship is not a matter of finding the right person, it's a matter of being the right person. That person is simply the pure you, being relentlessly, uncompromisingly, diligently you, not what you think anyone else expects, demands or wants of you. Then and only then will you offer your partner the gift that surpasses all others in your relationship—the perfect reflection in which they will see their own healing lessons.

You can tell when you're truly in love because you'll be allowing your loved one/s to be who they are without needing, wishing or trying to change them in any way. You'll also, however, absolutely allow yourself to be who you are—to be true to yourself— at all times, preferably without compromise and without stopping to think about it. That's the only way you can be positive that you're giving a loved one the true gift you'd spiritually promised to deliver—

reflecting to them exactly what they need to see for their own growth and healing. You'll always be living spontaneously by your own deepest truth for no other reason than pure love—self love—without analyzing it or controlling it or judging it.

Whatever another sees in you or feels about you as a result is exactly what their own Higher Self guides them to see to assist their own evolution, even if it's something they don't like.

Pure love lasts regardless of liking or disliking. Likes and dislikes are just ego reactions based on arbitrary and often ill founded beliefs. If you did stop to think about or try to rationally decide what you needed to reflect to another and just do that, you'd never be able to make the correct reflection because your ego would try to satisfy all manner of its own expectations and needs. What's more, it'd be trying to do so with only a fraction, if any, of the relevant knowledge and understanding of the Highest Good.

It must always be Higher Intelligence that guides both the reflection and the perception, and it communicates through your heart, not your head; through your inner sense, not your thoughts.

Surely it's better that, if a loved one feels hurt or upset, it's by the truth, not by a falsehood. Only in truth can full resolution and healing be completed. And the same goes for you—encourage your partner to always be true to themselves, and if ever you feel hurt it will at least be by the truth, not by lies. Then you'll have an honest and loving relationship rather than living a lie.

Look at your relationship and ask yourself a few basic questions to assess the quality of your love:

Do you love your partner enough to be truthful with them? Or do you love them enough to lie to them?

Do you love them enough to let them be themselves? Or do you love them enough to put a pressure on them to be someone they're not at ease (instead, dis-eased!) being?

It's your choice. It's always your choice, and until you're prepared to take your relationship through the white hot crucible of truth, it's healing gift will escape you both, as will true Love.

Disharmony or resistance in the giving and receiving of unconditional love—unconditional allowance and unconditional trust—will also reduce the ability of the body to heal many other diseases since the thymus, the gland of the heart chakra, is, spiritually speaking, your unfailing friend and colleague in the re-creation of tissues, cells, glands and organs that have fallen into disrepair. When the heart chakra is open and clear, this gland is fully active, ensuring that any part of your body can rebuild to match your perfect cosmic blueprint rather than your distorted 3D image of yourself.

It's not spiritual, holy, admirable or even helpful to denigrate your own happiness or wellbeing for the fear of how someone else might respond to you. It does nothing but lower your own vibration and compromise your self expression and eventually your health, not to mention your spiritual evolution and wellbeing. It thereby also reflects to others disease that they're harboring in their consciousness, compromises their energy and damages their vibration. That would be spiritually irresponsible on your part.

As beings who have committed to rediscover and live our God nature in a physical world, our challenge is to become sensitive to Cosmic Truth, which is neutral and objective, not to human subjective truth which is emotionally charged, warped and distorted by unconscious conditioning and biases.

Only with our heart's sensitivity will we begin to gain a deeper understanding of ourselves, our lives and our connectedness to the Source of all that is. Unbiased sensitivity is only accessible through an open heart chakra, a prerequisite for anyone willing to acknowledge and harmonize their own conditioning and prejudices, to heal and allow their true self to emerge, for their own benefit as well as for everyone else's.

Opening to life therefore requires that you allow the third chakra mental boundaries of your sensitivity, acceptability and receptiveness to break down, especially where they energetically divide your solar plexus (the highest of your three physical world chakras; the mental faculty) from your heart chakra (the allowing, sensitive bridge connecting the physical to the spiritual).

Opening your mind at its higher, spiritual boundary to more esoteric understandings and spiritual truths is the first step. Without that step, you'll remain trapped in what life has always represented (*re-presented*); trapped in the past. That's to say, locked in past cycles and patterns (conditions presented to you again and again), all of which weld you to the anvil of limitation and fear.

There is no judgment to be made on a life of limits; there's nothing wrong with it. I simply suggest that you self lovingly assess whether or not it's all you want your life to be. Does it serve you well? Does it support a vibrant and blissfully happy you? If so, then continue with it. If not, then changing it requires changing inside.

I for one, having traveled to dozens of countries around the world and encountered innumerable people from all walks of life, have yet to meet anyone who is content with every single minuscule stitch in the tapestry of their life. Whether in their physical world, their emotional experiences or in their mental state, they can find room for improvement. There appears always to be some degree of conflict or discontentment, often revealed in such sentiments as "I wish..." or "If only..." or "In a perfect world..."

If your joy and fulfillment is limited in any way at any time for any reason, no matter how slightly, then you're not living your full self or your full potential, you're living only a limited version of yourself and experiencing and benefiting from only a limited portion of your potential. To explore the rest of yourself requires opening to a higher perspective.

Figure 7

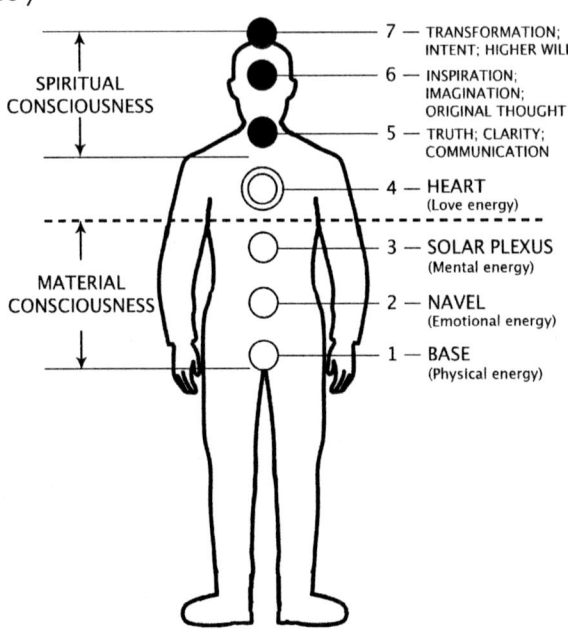

THE HIGHER CHAKRAS

Having opened your heart chakra and exposed yourself to such far reaching transformation of life and self, and with your life becoming awash with unconditionally loving experiences, people and attitudes, you'll still have more chakras in your body to open, clear and integrate consciously. *(Figure 7.)*

The Fifth Chakra

The throat chakra is the fifth—color tone blue; sound tone G. Attributes: truth and communication—putting it out as well as receiving it.

Your truth is different to mine. Our truths are as individual as our fingerprints and both are valid. There is conflict only when one person judges another, or themselves for that matter, to be right or wrong, or good or bad, or tries to make something or someone else mould to, accept or agree with their truth.

Take the aftermath of a crime. Invariably, eye-witness reports vary and only the consistent details would be considered beyond reasonable doubt. Yet each eyewitness reported their exact truth at the time. Anything is therefore truly as the beholder chooses to behold it, as any magician would agree.

Everyone has their own truth. We must all remember that another person's view is individual and to respect it as valid, whilst also respecting our own truth as equally valid. That they may differ simply adds to the richness of life. Adopting this viewpoint will assist in your personal healing by dissolving disease-causing judgment and bigotry in everyday life while strengthening and refining your own Inner Truth.

That's all very well, but how do you find your Inner Truth? We're so used to following what an outside authority tells us and accommodating the plethora of messages transmitted to us day in and day out that we've lost touch with our vital Inner Authority.

To rediscover that Inner Authority, you must open our heart in order to become sensitive to your own true feelings and subtle impulses and perceptions concerning anything and everything in your life. Only then are you able to discern in your heart what's true to you and what's not.

Because it involves sensitivity and subtle feeling, not rational thought, what most commonly confounds the discernment process is the influence of others; or should I say our tendency to allow the influence of others' views and preferences to overpower our own, This happens commonly because of our habit throughout life of relying largely on what's outside us.

What anyone else holds as their truth may or may not be the same as yours, but it doesn't need to be. As long as you value, trust and honor your own truth in your every action, thought, word and attitude, you'll become less inclined to find their truth a conflict or challenge. Instead you'll see it simply as being different, even a valuable alternative.

But if you do not know what's true to you, you can't live your truth, you can only live a lie or be a victim of someone else's truth. In that case, given time you'll forget your own truth ever existed and find yourself waiting with cap in hand for the next morsel of someone else's instruction, approval or permission before you'll feel okay about how you're living. And that's part of the present human predicament of animosity, resentment, judgment and conflict, not to mention the resultant violence which is based upon feeling like a victim with someone else pulling the strings in life.

When you pull the strings of your own life by developing ideas of what *you* want and being true to yourself, using that self knowledge as the motivation for everything you do, then outside influences will not upset you and you'll be taking responsibility for your own life. Your measure of fulfillment will increase immediately and dramatically and you'll be increasingly appreciative of and at ease with your life. Opportunities to achieve this self healing abound in everyday life. A typical instance comes to mind...

After years traveling, a daughter (I'll refer to her as Mary) returned home to visit her parents who were very proud of her worldly adventures. They'd arranged to take her as soon as possible to visit an elderly lonely friend of theirs whom they took care of, thinking the visit might brighten the friend's life a little. Mary had no real connection with the friend at all, never having even met them except once in her childhood. When asked to visit, she felt that other things were more important to her in the limited time of stay she had, so she declined. As it happencd, her parents had promised to visit their friend without consulting Mary. Unable to fulfill their self made promise, they became so upset about her refusal to mould to their wishes that an argument ensued leaving them upset, ill at ease and resentful.

If Mary had yielded to the outside influences of parental expectation and social convention instead of to her own Inner Truth about the situation, then she would have likely felt the need to suppress her frustration or resentment during the visit. Inevitably, that would entail suppressing her truth... just so as not to upset her parents or their friend or not to attract animosity or criticism. But, *"All of us could take a lesson from the weather—it pays no attention to criticism."* (Unknown origin).

Mary's situation is a simple example of her self love and living by self truth in a circumstance that was assumed to operate under the parents' or society's laws of control, conditioning, and overbearance in the seemingly innocent guise of social convention and family values.

If Mary had suppressed her truth, she would've been creating disease in herself, just to avoid spoiling others' comfort zones. Surely that's not self loving. Nor would it be loving of the parents to expect their daughter to become diseased in order to satisfy their own social conditioning and personal expectations.

It's easy to say "Oh, but just this once," but all of those 'just this once' occasions eventually add up to one enormous and acutely real healing issue which must be resolved some time by someone. And people's lives have become jam packed with the social debris of that mentality. It's much more beneficial for all concerned to nip it in the bud rather than to let it condense as disease. Mary's truth must be allowed out regardless of the result, as must her parents' truth.

Allowance of another's differing truth is vital if genuine love is to exist in a relationship. The only alternative is to force or coerce the other into submission... which is not love at all; it's control, the opposite of love. Love will always bring healing to the world whereas the seemingly harmless habit of living subtle lies can only fill the world with distortion and doubt and rebuild the old blankets of blindness to a higher vision and enlightened experience of life.

People have become convinced that they have to eliminate differences in order to keep the peace when in fact simple tolerance will achieve peace as well as disable judgment, and the criticisms that are its offspring, from creating disease throughout our world.

There seems to be a common assumption that eliminating differences will eliminate conflicts as well. But conflicts, like anger and judgment, are only within people, not within the differences themselves. The differences only enable people to feel conflict if they so choose. If people didn't have inner conflict concerning variety and uniqueness then diversity could exist harmoniously.

Removing differences doesn't remove conflict at all, it just suppresses it inside, inflaming people's victimhood attitudes and encouraging them to blame the outer world for the disharmony. This illustrates the elegant way in which the cosmos passively teaches us true wisdom by means of our everyday lives. Humankind will learn that only when its own attitudes of conflict and intolerance are eradicated can harmony exist in our world. That Truth will be learned only when people's ignorance and resistance to it creates enough pain for them stop avoiding the issue.

There's nothing wrong with being different to each other. It's only in little human minds, polarized by the habit of judgment, that one must be branded right and the other wrong; one assisted to win so that the other will lose; one be considered good and the other bad. We just need to know and accept that *different* is fine too. In fact, variety is vital to creation itself. For starters, it ensures we don't suffer a horribly homogenized world of sameness. (Or do we already?)

When differences are exposed in any circumstance, the situation is simply asking both parties to love each other enough to respect their differing truths. Peace can only happen by relinquishing the inner need or desire to change anything outside. That goes for people, families, communities, governments, religions and every other entity if they truly aspire to peace and not conflict.

Peace will never come about by trying to force others to yield or mould to something that's not fundamentally true to them. Only resentment and conflict will result... as usual. If you want to avoid conflict and disharmony in your life, stop wishing or trying to change others in any way, great or small. Acknowledge their truths and opinions as equally valid as your own without feeling the need to change theirs or yours but instead enjoying the diversity.

Apply discernment with your heart and you'll certainly become sensitive to what's true to you. Listen to your inner callings and impulses, not to outer influences or rules. What inspires you? What spontaneously *feels* right, even if it's not logical or rational? Your own healing will come about through communicating that Divinely inspired Inner Truth (throat chakra—5th) into your own life circumstances with love, compassion, trust and unconditionality (heart chakra—4th). It will then trickle down to influence your thoughts and attitudes and beliefs (solar plexus chakra—3rd), your emotions and your relationships with others (navel chakra—2nd), and even further into the actions you take (base chakra—1st) in each living moment. As above, so below.

In a nutshell, you'll be allowing your own Inner Truth to be the source of your life experiences and the motivation for who you are being, acting on it without hesitation, fear, compromise, guilt or regret. Until then you'll not know for sure whether your beliefs truly work for you or whether you need to modify them to heighten your life experience and expand your wisdom.

Bear in mind, though, that by modifying your truth I do not mean compromising it. I mean enabling it to evolve by letting go of obsolete beliefs or truths only when you feel you've encountered a higher truth or wisdom that inspires you to be more at peace with yourself, embrace more self power, self worth and confidence, and experience greater fulfillment, joy and love throughout your life.

Always modify your truth only in an upward, expansive direction, only in ways that engender higher frequency consciousness and greater fulfillment.

The Sixth Chakra

Inspiration is one of the traits of the next higher chakra—the brow; indigo; tone of A. Significant in its link with the pituitary gland, this is the center of insight, intuition, imagination, lateral thinking and access to potentiality and inspired ideas.

If, centuries ago, Leonardo da Vinci had not expressed the truth of what he imagined via his brow chakra and had the courage, self love and trust to communicate it both verbally and actively, mankind would not have had that early introduction to such remarkable, revolutionary concepts as the helicopter, the parachute or hydraulics. If it weren't for others of similar inspired courage then we'd also have continued to believe that the world is flat, the planets revolve around the Earth and we have little or no say in our own lives.

Indeed, we can attribute human progress to this chakra since it enables us to imagine and perceive outside the status quo constraints, conditioning and blind acceptance of what *appears* to be real. Instead it enables us to explore the endless ocean of infinite potentiality from and into which the stream of creation flows.

Any time you want to expand your opportunities or possibilities, the ideas come to you via your brow chakra. You can then allow them to trickle down to guide all your earthly levels of expression until you put them into action and enjoy their material benefits.

The sixth chakra also plays a vital role in conjunction with the seventh. Their associated glands, the pineal (7th) and pituitary (6th), act like the adjacent faces at the point of a prism, splitting pure life force energy (as white light) into its individual constituent parts to enable us to exist in a body and experience life through the energy structuring nature of the chakra system. *(Figure 8.)*

Figure 8

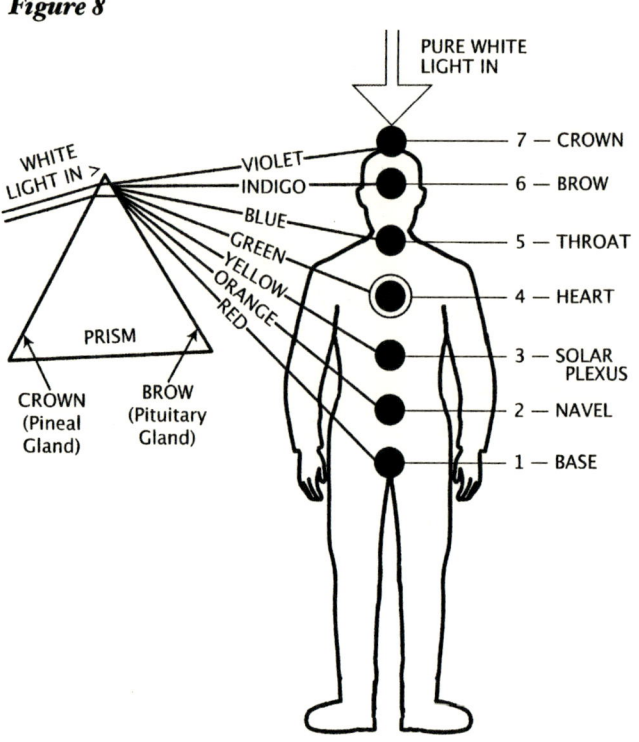

PURE WHITE LIGHT IN

WHITE LIGHT IN

VIOLET
INDIGO
BLUE
GREEN
YELLOW
ORANGE
RED

PRISM

CROWN (Pineal Gland)

BROW (Pituitary Gland)

7 — CROWN
6 — BROW
5 — THROAT
4 — HEART
3 — SOLAR PLEXUS
2 — NAVEL
1 — BASE

Consequently, this portal is further responsible for directing the correct frequencies and intensities of life force energy to the various parts of the body and managing your body's operating temperature by way of the pituitary gland. Being our *third eye*, it also facilitates the ability to 'see' beyond the obvious outer appearance of life's circumstances and sense the subtle inner reality of the forces governing consciousness, energy, auras and the chakras themselves.

The Seventh Chakra

The uppermost of the chakras in the physical body is the seventh—the crown. It's at the top of your head and resonates to the color violet and the sound tone B. This chakra is your interdimensional gateway into higher realms of consciousness. It's the highest chakra we can fully integrate whilst still being able to choose a physical form since only seven main portals are contained within the body.

Opening this portal to a greater flow of life force energy provides your earthly self, via your Higher Self, direct access to the wisdom and messaging of the Supreme Intelligence, as well as access to the sublime dimensions of life, existence and creation. The condition of this chakra determines our ability to advance even higher in our spiritual evolution. In conjunction with the pineal gland, the crown chakra is vital in our ability to both maintain our entire life force field, and create the life we want so dearly, instead of the limited one we thought we were stuck with.

The chakra system doesn't stop at the seventh. It's an infinite extension of portals constantly exchanging increasingly high frequencies of energy, enabling and nourishing life on all levels of consciousness to exist. The seven major energy portals described are the extent of frequencies that can be encapsulated in physical human form as we know it in the dense levels of consciousness.

To extend further requires that the body and its energy architecture undergo extensive transformation and development to accommodate the higher frequencies whilst sustaining physical form. In accordance with the principle of highest frequency represents the highest expression of self, your highest expression is determined by the quality and purity of connection you maintain, by your own free will and discipline, with your own soul essence and with the source of all consciousness via your seventh chakra and Higher Self.

In our world of being physical, the highest expression of self means manifesting the life that the soul had intended. That is, mutually exercising our individual free will to deliberately create our own reality with little or no interference from our self limiting patterns, biases and conditioning or from outside influences that can never know our own Inner Voice nor our own unique path to self realization.

Creative Duo

Together, the sixth and seventh chakras share another crucial function in human consciousness, a function more far reaching than many people give them credit for—creation itself. These portals are directly related to the essential qualities of our receptive (passive/ feminine) and projective (active/ masculine) principles. The pituitary and pineal glands respectively handle these attributes and interact in unique ways with the right and left hemispheres of the brain to ensure that we have absolute free will to determine what we experience.

FREE WILL

The principle of free will is fundamental to our consciousness, our life purpose and our existence. Not even the Godhead itself, the highest Source of all that is, will encroach upon our free will under *any* circumstances. After all, that's the very intelligence that arranged everything so that we'd have the power of free will in the first place.

And what is this free will? It's the freedom to will for ourselves whatever we choose. Without compromises or limits, every person has the freedom to choose whatever they put their thoughts and attention on, which will unquestionably become energized by the force of creation through them to become their experience. Yet, even when made clear to them, this gift of supreme power continues to be rejected or denied by most people.

Why? Because many are happier maintaining a victim role than taking responsibility for the sovereignty they actually have over their entire reality. Others look at their life and can't stand to admit that they have made the choices they have nor believe they'd ever have created such things for themselves to experience. They all prefer to blame for their predicaments some outside influence... but nevertheless an influence to which they—nobody else—chose to succumb.

Free will doesn't mean that we get whatever we want, it only ensures that we get whatever we focus the most attention upon. Though physical effort and emotional energy contribute enormously to the creation process, thought energy is especially what directs the flow since that's at the highest level of our 3D realm. It's closer to the source of the creation cycle.

I'm sure people would not have focused their attention upon pain, struggle, poverty or any other unpleasantness had they known the power of their thoughts to manifest as experiences. They'd have focused upon other things, no doubt. We didn't become aware earlier of this ultimate spiritual power within us all because had we learned of it and practiced and mastered its potential to even the slightest degree, we'd have never been at the mercy of controllers and power mongers the way we historically have, and masses still are.

Only when people become awakened to this basic spiritual Truth and become allowing enough to accept it, and proceed to discipline their normally scattered and distracted minds will they break free from the relentless bombardment of undesirable experiences and circumstances in their lives. That's genuine empowerment. It's authentic freedom. It's breaking free of the wheel of karma; transcending pain and limitation.

Karma is not punishment nor retribution; it's simply what we experience as a result of past actions. Karma is the consequences of the Creation Force. The problem is that, having such gross 3D impressions, it's been too easy all along to assume that actions are only physical.

But Creation Force applies to all actions and the consequences that are least obvious and we're least prepared for are based upon *thought* actions in the form of consistent beliefs, mental images and attitudes. Also contributing in this subtle creation machinery are *emotional* actions, in the form of the strongest feelings and conditioned reactions that we choose to perpetuate in our lives. Less subtly, our physical actions which the most obvious consequences.

The way a person chooses to view this principle of karma has no bearing whatsoever on how it affects their life. It's irrelevant whether you believe it or not, or use it or abuse it. This is immutable Cosmic Law functioning inside and outside our universe. It doesn't make decisions or choices for us nor answer our ego's petulant whims and cries. It simply serves the greater principles of creation by which we function, with or without our knowledge of it. Also, being universal, it prevails over human-concocted earthly laws that really only serve the vested interests of a power-drunk and control-desperate minority.

Surely it's not difficult to see that *everyone* has absolute free will to think anything they choose. Though they might be able to convince or influence you, nobody can *force* you to think anything. If they tried, you could just say you will but then focus on something completely different without them ever knowing. When you're ready and willing to master yourself and your life, then you'll accept that karma—

the Cosmic Law of Creation—ensures that you *will* sooner or later experience whatever you focus your thoughts and emotions, energy and attention upon. Whether it's what you want or what you don't want it, whether it's your own idea or someone else's that you've accepted, you'll get it.

Always focus your attention on things you want to experience more of and appreciate in life. Make a list of things in your life now that you do appreciate and want, and allow your mind to ponder and dwell on them in your quiet times. Additionally, dream up a list of things you'd like to experience in the future sometime. Any time you feel down or disappointed, read the lists through over and over to remind yourself of these things. No matter how insignificant they may seem now, if they attract the majority of your attention then they, and things like them, will fill the majority of your future.

Your pineal and pituitary glands play a vital role in this creation process, receiving and transmitting images via the thalami, which act like TV screens in your head. The pituitary gland receives onto one screen unconscious images (which people call psychic or intuitive, imagination or ideas) while the pineal gland projects onto the other TV screen conscious images (which people call 'rational'). The conscious images become the seeds of your experiential world, the thought forms that are energized to materialize in physical form.

The source of these thought forms can be anything but we depend largely on two. The most common and influential is the brain, which receives its most direct information from your physical reality through your five main senses: sight, sound, touch, taste and smell.

In the case of someone being unaware of their inner creation mechanism, this sensory information constitutes almost all of the images projected onto the pineal gland's TV screen. But the other main source, more significantly, takes us back to the pituitary gland. It receives thought forms or ideas onto its own TV screen projected from the infinite, non-physical stream of Supreme Intelligence and potentiality that lies beyond what *appears* to be real in our world. The thought forms and ideas from this source often have little or no rational base yet are responsible for remarkable inventions and advancements in human evolution. This second TV screen gives us intuitive flashes and bright ideas to evaluate and, if we so choose, consciously put onto the other TV screen to become created in our lives. These images however are not as robust as those from the five gross senses since they're often fleeting and subtle, so people tend not to notice or heed them.

You could think of this process as the Universal Flow of Creation constantly feeding one TV screen (pituitary) with possibilities for you to choose from whilst at the same time watching the other screen (pineal) to see which possibilities you are most interested in and give most attention to, and then faithfully reproducing those for you.

The difference between the two screens is whatever

you omit to transfer from the pituitary to the pineal screen, which Creation assumes you've chosen not to accept and therefore not experience. It just continues looking at what's on your conscious, intentional TV screen (what occupies your thoughts the most) and produces that in form. Hey presto! Whatever you think about, you get.

It stands to reason then that if you're always preoccupied by your present outer reality, you'll continue to get more of it. Without exception, if you've been diligently and clearly thinking of something for some time yet it's not materializing anywhere in your life then it's time to ask yourself if you're actually imagining it 'over here' with you or 'over there' with someone else. Always imagine what you want as already being 'over here' with you. As well, check out if you've been putting more thought attention on it than any of the other innumerable distractions in life.

When you use your imagination to dream up things you'd love to experience and when you're willing to open to life force and higher consciousness, you allow remarkable concepts and thoughts to enter your own personal creation factory that determines your life.

Before you know it, this new influence of the remarkable and *un*-real begins to materialize as real miracles in your life. Think of what you'd love; dream about beautiful things; whatever you wish. But try not to let yourself be convinced or distracted by your outside reality. Your inside reality precedes your experience, it doesn't follow it.

Unfortunately, this system of evolution is presently

almost disabled because the pituitary gland is inactive or ignored in most people. This is due to their habit of disregarding higher principles or the spiritual considerations of life plus accepting the belief that they have no power over their own life.

It's a disease that's plagued humankind since time immemorial. Consequently, the images received by the brain and energized for creation come largely from the five senses, all of which are dedicated solely to what's existing in your own reality—your limited personal slice of the material world's infinite potential.

The material world gives you only your personal impression of what reality can be, the senses relating only to and confirming only that image, faithfully feeding the existing picture back into your thought machinery. So you keep thinking it's *the* reality rather than just one possible reality. This overwhelms all the more subtle and frail newborn ideas and thoughts and is therefore the set of thoughts that gets energized and created. Or should I say, *re*-created... over and over again.

As you can see, a cycle is established, a loop set up whereby the way you see and relate to your present reality is by far the strongest influence on what you create as a future reality. Same mentality, same reality. Because you're preoccupied by your existing life circumstances, your existing reality becomes perpetuated, or at least appears exceedingly difficult and/or painstakingly slow to change. Sound familiar?

To kick your creative powers out of that repetitive loop of 'the same old stuff' and into 'un-same new stuff' requires that the sixth chakra be activated, heeded and trusted. It will then begin to energize and kick start what was otherwise a consistently preoccupied pituitary gland just needing some new energy directed to it.

The simplest and possibly most effective method, though it can take some time, is meditation. In meditation you defocus the five primary physical senses, temporarily rendering them inactive, or at least ineffectual. This makes a huge difference to the type of information being processed by the brain and therefore also to the thought forms creating your life through the pineal and pituitary glands. Sight consists the vast majority of your sensory input and sound the next most significant portion. Next is touch, and the remainder comprises smell and taste.

If you close your eyes and sit still in a quiet place these senses receive little or no input. If you stay awake while the senses are starved of information in this way, you create the state of meditation. In this way, the meditative state creates an enormous vacuum in the stream of rational day-to-day thinking. Your mind, normally occupied with mundane 'mind fill' from the five gross senses, can become distressed at the unfamiliar emptiness and begin filling the vacuum with spurious thoughts and ramblings from its own store of recent memories and current experiences. If you find your mind chattering when you begin meditating (which most people do), you're experiencing the effects of this normal response.

However the cosmos, by nature, doesn't sustain

a vacuum. So when you become adept at the mental stillness of meditation, you create for yourself the opportunity for extraordinary things from outside your normal realm of possibilities to flow in and displace the ordinary.

This subtler interdimensional energy will probably not at first be recognizable by the rational mind as thought forms or even as sense because it's coming from higher frequencies of consciousness that the mind is not used to translating, much the same way as the human eye will not see ultraviolet or infrared light because their frequencies are outside our normal range of optical sensitivity.

Persevere with a regime of staying awake while denying the brain its usual overdose of outer-sensory information, and it gets tired of looking for or generating spurious mental dross to fill the space. It begins to look for alternative stimulus and finds the information that sneaks in through the pineal and pituitary glands from the greater pool of Cosmic Intelligence.

The brain's pathways of input, having become quiet and empty of the overbearing outside reality, begin to fill with the new, more subtle higher frequencies as thoughts, images or concepts. This intuitive messaging is not even perceived by the usual mind, but nevertheless it gradually begins to guide and influence your thoughts.

At first this happens in very subtle, unnoticeable ways but eventually with your full awareness of it. Most significantly, the new thoughts influence what you're pumping out through your personal creation machinery and your experience of life begins to change as a result.

The more you notice, listen to and act upon the input from higher consciousness from your subtle Inner Voice, in the form of enlightened attitudes and fresh ideas, intuitive flashes, impulses and urges, the stronger its influence becomes.

This influence that nudges you in subtle ways through life is what most people think of as spirit guides or what others refer to as their gut feel. The stronger this influence becomes through your Higher Self's lofty vibrations, the more clearly you're guided through life according to a higher purpose and meaningful direction. More than that, the faster your reality rises in vibration to become filled with love and unconditionality, joy and fulfillment, abundance and wellbeing; qualities that had previously only existed in your life's unseen *potentiality* but which you'll have begun to allow into your actual *reality*.

These are some of the reasons I use meditation techniques to help people activate and open their energy channels and chakras in my workshop called Cosmic Activation (see last page). It's developed specifically to facilitate willing people's opening to channel; that is, opening to life. During the workshop, participants invariably experience the impact of integrating new higher frequencies of energy into their old lower frequency energy system, physical body and consciousness.

When deliberately opened with proper knowing and

preparation, the energy field is able to receive a massive influx of life force energy that could have otherwise overwhelmed the person without suitable grounding. That is exactly what happened to me when I returned from the jetty with Michael all those years ago. It would never endanger anyone but could easily disturb them as its effects can destabilize their otherwise familiar state of consciousness. These effects are not usually helpful to the process of spiritual growth since they normally produce a degree of doubt or apprehension in the person—more resistance which will inevitably have to be dissolved. It certainly produced doubt and apprehension in me, but the overriding sense of euphoria drew me on and sustained my acceptance of the experience, rather than my resistance to it.

The mere fact that a person attends my Cosmic Activation workshop of their own free will serves greatly in eliminating this disturbance since their consciousness begins subtly preparing for opening the channels. The instant they make their commitment to attend, inner messaging awakens their own perfect methodology. That innate process uses the activities and environment of the workshop to achieve the perfect result for their highest good—openness to the higher forces of Light.

THE TRUTH ABOUT CHANNELING

I do not intend this book to be a guide to human consciousness and life purpose. For that I recommend that you read my book entitled *From Atoms to Angels* (ISBN: 0-908807-11-2). In it is a full description of how the gross physical body and the subtle energy bodies interact within the overall scheme and purpose of our existence.

I shall however briefly reiterate one of the book's basic premises that the life force energy comes from higher vibrational levels, methodically stepping down its frequency through a series of contained dimensions, or realms of consciousness. Each dimension is a unique band of energy frequencies spanning awareness and life according to the attributes of its particular spectrum.

The spectrum that contains us humans is called the third dimension because occupying it are the life forms of three dimensional consciousness and lower, as I've described earlier in these pages.

As far as we humans are concerned, when the energy enters our physical spectrum we're able to be aware of it; to experience, perceive, detect, integrate and even study it as all matter and phenomena in our universe, ourselves and our lives. The energy also enters the form of our physical human body and enlivens it, making it a usable vehicle for us to function and gather experience as physical creatures in our earthly domain.

Plainly, we're conduits, or channels for the cosmic

life force energy to flow into our dense type of reality. But that's not the point I wish to make. I want to make it absolutely clear that we cannot *exist* without it because we *are* it and it's all we experience. If we were not channels for higher energy and consciousness, we simply would not exist.

Being a channel is the most natural and vital thing we do. It would be totally unnatural, even detrimental, to refuse to channel higher consciousness as Light and energy. Our ultimate purpose in the cosmos is to channel the life force energy in the purest form possible from the higher realms of consciousness into ours.

As the new consciousness on our planet has begun to emerge and gain momentum, increasingly there has developed misunderstanding and conjecture concerning the phenomenon of people allowing aspects of higher vibrational consciousness to communicate through them into our realm, some verbally and others in written form. Unfortunately, the assumptions and hearsay have enabled, even encouraged some people who channel in these ways to develop bloated self impressions and to believe themselves to be something special because of their channeling.

Let me state absolutely categorically that ANYONE can channel. In fact EVERYONE does so already. It's not the exclusive domain of a blessed few, nor is it some unique power with which only a handful of individuals are fortunate enough to be born. Your life simply couldn't have existed without you channeling in some way or other. If you stopped channeling, you'd die. It's that simple.

Everyone channels. The issue is therefore not one of 'To channel or not to channel,' it's only a matter of purity—faithfulness to the original vibration of the energy. How far up the ladder are you willing to connect?

How you use your channeling is up to you and your free will. You're already channeling by being alive... by eating and talking, thinking and feeling and sleeping and interacting in all of life's ways. If you want to also begin using your channeling for voice or written interdimensional transmissions from other realms, then just be aware that it requires you plugging in directly at a higher point up the frequency ladder, exposing you to higher intensities of energy.

To channel clearly necessitates almost completely bypassing the lower three chakras of physical, emotional and mental influence since they're the realm of the ego.

This is a challenge that raises all manner of dilemmas and questions within since what differentiates the favored 'clear channel' from a blocked (ego-infected) channel is the degree to which they keep their conscious physical, emotional and mental influences removed from any transmission. The higher their degree of detachment concerning the outcome of the transmission, the less ego interference and clearer they channel.

Invariably this will also be demonstrated in their detached attitude towards life in general; that is, being present and involved in everyday life but motivated and guided only by their deepest truths and principles.

Without hesitation or caution, I encourage you to proceed. I personally wish that everyone would channel more clearly the wisdom of the higher orders of intelligence every moment of every day; it would positively transform the world overnight.

Because of the unpredictability and the inner effects of clear channeling, I also encourage you to ask yourself how detached you are concerning what comes of it. Are you willing to channel into your life the purest forms of the energy whatever adjustments that may bring? How much transformation are you willing to undergo in your life? What form are you willing to allow the channeling to take; direct voice, energy healing, creative activities or pure self awareness and honesty? Are you willing to stand back and allow yourself to be involved in the process in every moment of your life without hesitation or compromise, regardless of the results? Are you truly willing to put aside your own conditioning, biases and any expectations to allow the unpredictable and extraordinary to come about in you and your life and through your channeling?

The channeling phenomenon triggers fear in many people. Actually, more often than not it's just the idea of channeling with its unknown, misunderstood and misrepresented nature that arouses their fear and resistance. But that fear is only of the unknown and how it might affect their comfort zone or conflict with their way of thinking or living. Some of the most noted (and widely quoted) clear channels in known history include Buddha and Jesus.

You can't avoid the fact that the more purely aligned you are with the source energy, the more your life will become transformed and the more others around you will be affected. After all, everything you be and do and experience is a direct reflection of the channeling (living) you've done to date. When you've resisted or distorted the channeled energy and its effects, it has manifested as diseased, difficult, conflicting and toxic circumstances in life.

When you open to channel more purely, you open to life as a completely different set of circumstances. Changing from one set of life circumstances to another can be disturbing and disruptive. But that just makes it uncomfortable, not harmful or dangerous as some suggest. How can anything bring danger when it comes from the Supreme Source of all life itself? I find the notion laughable.

Any danger lies not in the energy itself but in how it's used or abused, interpreted, filtered or distorted, and that's invariably and unquestionably the sole responsibility of the channel, not of the energy. The energy is at the mercy of our will as it enters our realm through us. This explains why things happen in our world that people can't believe or accept would have been the 'Will of God.' In fact they're not. They're the pure Will of God tainted by the misguided impure will of human egos.

Everyone always has free will, an irrevocable gift and power in life which we must learn to exercise in a manner that upholds our highest consciousness, our spiritual growth and our Supreme Purpose.

The plethora of new understanding and guidance pouring into our global consciousness through written and vocal forms of the channeling phenomenon is just one sign of great change that's upon us; a phenomenal swing towards alternative understanding and answers which can facilitate higher consciousness and essential purpose in each of our personal lives.

It's certainly not required that you accept all the channeled information as being true to you but, if you're to rise into the state of love, harmony and mastery, you are required to *allow it to be*. Whether you personally agree with it or not, just allowing that the information may serve someone else or another time or place helps keep you in the state of higher love energy.

Channeled information is sometimes meaningless at the time of its transmission yet is part of a larger picture that hasn't yet taken meaningful form. There's also plenty of channeled material that's nothing more than a person using or feigning the activity of channeling to vent their own personal will or to try and coerce others to support them. It's your responsibility not to police or judge this but to remain detached so that you can discern whether or not any channeled transmission rings true to you or feels important for you.

You're only asked to accept what elevates our sense of self worth, empowerment, purpose, love and fulfillment in any given instant. You need only accept what you discern is true to you or *feel* strikes an unmistakable "Yes" cord deep within, irrespective of any other person's influence or response to it. Anything else can just be ignored, allowed to exist but not paid attention to or accepted as relevant guidance. If it's something you ignore now but higher intelligence brings it for your highest good, then you can rest assured it will be brought to your attention again somehow, sometime, somewhere. You'll never lose anything that's vital to your wellbeing or evolution by exercising discernment.

At all times, irrespective of the circumstances you're faced with in life, remain skeptical whilst maintaining an open mind. Don't ever be gullible by blindly accepting everything or even accepting what someone else approves of. Your Inner Truth must always give you the nod; listen only to the *feeling* that it's for you.

No channeled information you receive is correct or incorrect until you *feel* that it is. Getting to know those feelings, not emotional reactions or mental judgments, so that they can guide you properly is your own responsibility.

The validity of transmitted or received channeled energy in any form is all about being nonresistant whilst at the same time exercising your personal responsibility for the choices you're making. You choose what to accept out of all that's available in life, and channeling should be no different. Though others may try to coerce or even force your choice in some way, it's always you who ultimately chooses whether to follow or disregard their influence.

You're the one who must put out into the world a stream of consciousness that's uniquely yours and is deeply true to you or otherwise suffer the compromises to which you agree. Only you can choose to allow or to warp the essential perfection of the energy as you go about your chosen path in life. It's also you who is responsible for maintaining your allowing attitude towards the unique path through life that any other soul may choose, whether it agrees with you personally or not.

Ultimately, you're responsible for all of your choices, whether you choose to listen to outside influences or to be guided by your own Inner Truth and senses.

It's not uncommon to encounter people who decry the phenomenon of channeling per se, just because there is something about it they don't like or or can't accept, or with which they personally don't agree.

To decry channeling, though, is about as rational as condemning all trees because you didn't like the flavor of the last apple you ate. Channeling has always been around, the essence of life, not to mention of all spiritual and religious teachings.

For that reason there are also those who profess that today's form of channeling is just a hyped up, glorified, or re-labeled version of the age old activities of the great prophets and disciples of every culture; what the gurus of the East have done for centuries; what the traditional psychic mediumship of the spiritualist church movement has used in the more recent past to communicate with the dead.

I understand that these phenomena are the same, but only to the extent that they represent a physical human being offering themselves as a conduit for non-physical realms of consciousness. There the similarity ends. I'll explain.

In the case of the great spiritual leaders and disciples, the intention was to be a channel for the beings of the higher dimensions of Supreme or Cosmic Intelligence to telepathically communicate genuine wisdom interdimensionally so that people in our world could learn and evolve in a way that supported their highest good and higher purpose. These beings have never inhabited a physical body, having always dwelt in realms of Light and pure consciousness.

In the case of the spiritualist movement, mediums have been enabling the non-physical frequencies of *human* consciousness—people who have died and become disembodied spirits, or discarnate beings—to contact our world of embodiment. The motive in their case was to rekindle the awareness of life continuing after physical death. That was a vital function in the western population who had become spiritually bereft through rigid, misleading and disempowering religious dogma, control and fear mongery.

However, just because a being is not physical doesn't mean they're of higher consciousness, nor that their motives are any more holy or loving than any physical person you might encounter. Many supporters of this phenomenon are simply enchanted by the idea of a wiser ancient or ethnic culture wanting to contact them or by the attraction of glamorizing their own past in some way to vindicate or explain their present.

When you look deeper, those two phenomena— channeling and psychic mediumship—are quite different based on the knowledge that we're now in a world of somewhat different energy and consciousness.

The fact that the overall vibrational rate, or quality, of human consciousness has been rising, particularly over the last couple of thousand years, means we've been able to evolve by withstanding exposure to higher and higher frequencies and greater quantities and intensities of life force energy without blowing our switchboards.

This intensified life force is evidenced by the signs of 'more life' in our world—longer life spans, more activity on the planet, more variety and choice, more immediate experiences and the expectation of immediate gratification, not to mention all the infrastructure, technological developments, education and communications that enable it to take place.

So the channeling of this day and new age I prefer to call *interdimensional telepathy* since it's the transfer of concepts and understanding through a flow of energy between fundamentally different dimensions of consciousness. I use the term with the intention of being accurate rather than convoluted or special in any way.

Interdimensional telepathy allows into our awareness energies from distinctly different dimensional realms of consciousness, energies of higher intelligence that, uncompromised by past physical experience, can offer us a fresh and pure perspective on life; wisdom vital to our evolution through these changing times. It's capable of bringing us a higher perspective that's inspirational and can guide us out of our limited view of our life and our potential and into a new framework of understanding and being, a totally new context for living.

This channeling phenomenon can and ultimately will facilitate complete opening to life—the emergence of true personal power and freedom for one and all instead of continuing powerlessness, limitation, judgment, conflict, scarcity and victimhood. As such, it's more aligned to the spiritual masters of millennia past who have been repeatedly recorded as influencing everyone around them, even by their sheer presence without saying a word.

Channeling in this day and new age is of the same ilk. It's really the *energy* that makes the difference. The energy transmitted through this interdimensional telepathy is of greater service to our evolution than the actual words being spoken or written.

It's as though the words come riding in on the energy like leaves on a river, there to entertain and distract the rational minds of listeners. The analytical left brain that wants to know things would otherwise interrupt and interfere with the process by trying to figure out, contradict or question the unknown and unpredictable data. But the underlying energy itself washes over and through everyone present, raising their personal consciousness vibration by sheer exposure to the higher vibrational energy.

However, mediumship—channeling the discarnate spirits of people who have physically died—serves only to prove life after physical death. But the human personalities being channeled are still within our 3D reality, just minus their flesh-and-bone form. They're basically auras without bodies, so they still retain all the judgmental or biased human conditioning, controls and limitations that their mental and emotional bodies had when they were physical.

Their non physical nature certainly doesn't endow them with any higher consciousness or wisdom than they had before, and probably no higher than us who are still in the flesh. They can contribute to our evolution little or nothing more than their own personal views and opinions that are still trapped in their subtle bodies of emotional and mental energy. They no doubt can offer a different perspective on our existence, but it will inevitably be compromised by their residual human conditioning.

An attendee in one of my Cosmic Activation workshops once said "If they didn't how much an apple cost before they died, they sure don't know after." That sums it up.

Just because someone is not in a physical body doesn't mean they're of higher intelligence or consciousness; nor does it necessarily mean they're coming from a healthy or higher intention.

In practical terms, you can tell the difference between these two distinct channeling modalities quite easily. Through traditional mediumship you'll generally get a variation on the theme of existing human perceptions and ideas, often interlaced with opinions and judgments—the should's and could's, ought to's and ought not's, goods and bads, rights and wrongs of 3D consciousness. A flow of historical data or information directly derived from the material plane, albeit with a twist in perspective, is also often on the menu.

This is because that form of mediumship takes place through the solar plexus—the center of the human mental body. It therefore resonates with human mental energy and expresses only within the medium's personal framework and capacity of mental understanding and thinking. This is inevitably governed by their own personal beliefs, conditioning, biases and human-ness because that's what the energy is able to resonate, connect and blend with in the human channel.

That's why the most remarkable mediums of times gone by, such as the famous Edgar Cayce, worked in a trance state whereby the ordinary limited knowledge of their ego mind was less inclined to interfere with the information being transmitted. They didn't 'listen in' to check and interfere with the transmission of information that they didn't intellectually know themselves.

Interdimensional telepathy, on the other hand, makes available to us the higher wisdom of beings who have either never fallen to the depths of consciousness that we presently inhabit or they have learned to rise out of it through self realization and integration of higher realms of wisdom and consciousness, not by conventional death. But they have most often never been physical.

Their consciousness resides permanently in the realms of intelligence and life which, with their full knowledge and intention, are integrated with the

Source of all that is—the Godhead; Supreme Mind; whatever you wish to call it.

They do not behave with conditionality, fear, judgment, control, conflict or limitations with which human consciousness is plagued. They respect the Cosmic Law of free will so never tell anyone what to do, what to believe or think, what's right or wrong, or good or bad. They offer choices as to what you may believe, how you may choose to make changes and live, how you may understand yourself and manifest your potential, heal and rediscover your innate God nature.

These higher realms of intelligence will never attempt to force or coerce you into believing anything

Figure 9

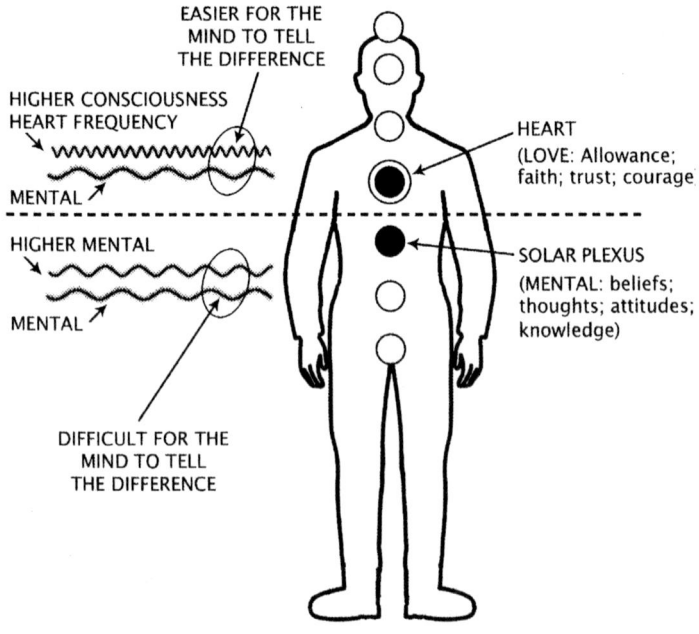

or doing anything. Seldom will they even try to convince you because they're not interested in proselytizing, only in liberating human potential and pure Divine nature *by our free choice*; guiding our highest evolution into reunion with the Supreme Intelligence and unlimited fulfillment by our own free will.

When all is said and done, it's still vital that you listen to, accept or follow only what resonates deeply with your own Inner Truth. Nothing else. After all, why should you treat channeled information any differently than something your neighbor or friend says? It's just communication and it's always up to you what you do with it and how you respond to it.

The wisdom of a Divine perspective, I'm sure you'd agree, will inevitably be somewhat different to human understanding from an Earthly perspective. It therefore has a greater potential to guide us out of our present troubles and into higher states of consciousness and existence.

The fact that Higher Wisdom transmits on a higher frequency of energy using the heart chakra instead of the solar plexus chakra also puts it on a *different wavelength* from the channel's own mental energy. *(Figure 9.)* This greatly reduces the problem of interference by the channel since they're better able to distinguish their own mind's activities from the channeled information. As well, their thinking mind is less able to spontaneously interpret and react to the transmission.

This frequency differential creates a situation whereby the person channeling either loses the connection and stops the transmission or they sustain the connection and let the transmission flow with minimum interference. Either way, the integrity of the wisdom is preserved to the maximum degree.

Though what the channeling conveys doesn't necessarily seem rational or meaningful at times, the higher consciousness will still have its effect through its energy alone, by osmosis, like steam melting ice, irrespective of the actual words.

People who directly experience this channeling phenomenon often *feel* the energy, in ways they can't put into words. They may feel inspired, uplifted or empowered, often with a sense of confirmation of some issues and curiosity concerning others. Some people get a deep sense of joy or even become moved to channel something themselves as become flooded with the energy.

I remember an occasion in Hong Kong when the pure effect of the channeled energy far outshone the words being transmitted. It was June 1993 and I was conducting a large meditation group where I regularly channeled the Ascended Masters. Early in the channeled transmission, the room full of people erupted into laughter for more than half an hour until the channeled transmission was over, at which time the laughter subsided. I always recorded the channeled portion of the evenings so that I too could listen to the words later since I did not know what I was channeling at the time. When I later listened to the recording of that evening's transmission by Master Merlin, there was nothing funny in the words.

Nothing. The wild laughter was the result solely of the uplifting energy of the transmission.

Laughter opens the heart, which is exactly what the Higher Intelligence wants to achieve with us and exactly what they achieved on that occasion through the channeled *energy*, not by words.

Interdimensional telepathy, simultaneously translated almost unconsciously by a willing and open channel into human communications, is the mode of channeling from which you can glean gems of true wisdom—options for how you might view, understand, transform or develop your life and to realize your own higher potential; understanding of the state of humanity and the world; ways that you might choose to become of service to the evolution of humankind and the planet; previously unimagined roles you can fill in service to Divine Light and the manifestation of the Plan Of Light—Heaven On Earth; Nirvana; an empowered and spiritually mature species and planet.

Usually, anybody exposed to channeled energies feels the effects physically at the time—itching, heat or chill, 'butterflies' in the stomach, shaking or vibrating in their body, feeling unable to move, or unable to stay still, for that matter. Some experience spontaneous emotional releases of tears or laughter or hear ringing or buzzing in their head or even get headaches during the channeling which disappear immediately it finishes. Others get vivid images or thoughts coming to mind or get a strong "Aha!" concerning some important issue in their life. As well as endless other sensations, these are all just symptoms of unfamiliar raw energy flooding into a person and disturbing their otherwise familiar patterns of feelings, thoughts and sensations.

Though its content and effects may be disruptive or bewildering at times, this channeling phenomenon is not just meddling with life. On the contrary, it's the ever intensifying influx of fresh, unadulterated consciousness that's able to alter the way humanity evolves in most fulfilling and empowering ways.

It'll do exactly that, should we be willing to open to the potentiality of its guidance and become relentlessly responsible and discerning about what affects the choices we make on a daily basis; as long as we're willing to acknowledge and accept the myriad effects of the energy in our own lives—signs that we're opening to life.

SIGNS OF LIFE

As I've explained, channeled energy is the basic substance of all experience and all reality; no exceptions.

All form and actions (physical energy), memory and re-actions (emotional energy), thoughts and beliefs (mental energy), trust, faith, courage, detachment and allowance (love energy), communication, clarity and peace (truth energy), and imagination, ideas and inspiration (intuitive energy) are segments of the infinite spectrum of energy frequencies that make up human consciousness. Each segment is defined by the particular range of frequencies it's occupying and works through one or another of the main energy portals, or chakras, in the human body.

All phenomena, objects, substances and types of materiality, along with their functions, are also manifestations of the same life force energy, just in different vibrations.

You could say that this is why God is described not as an individual being but as an omnipresent and omnipotent, formless and nameless presence or force. The concept has generally been quite difficult to accept due to human consciousness being so obsessed by the 3D limitations and perceptions, polarity and separateness. Anything with a label—even God—we believe must have a form or it's can't be real.

But in truth, the essential Life Force energy takes infinite different forms since it is the actual energy that comprises the whole of existence.

The channeled life force energy becomes more

potent and accessible depending on what we do with our life. Healing, vocal channeling, spiritual counseling and guidance, body work, energy work and all esoteric activities typically encourage the energy and its manifestations. This is because when a person has the intention to use their life in service to higher realization and empowerment in such ways, they have automatically opened themselves to the potential of the higher frequencies of energy that those activities employ. The person's physical actions are less removed from and more closely connected to the source of the energy. So when you open to life, you increase your life force energy and these activities become more pure, empowered and effective.

The only limitations on the energy are those we put upon it—our own will, tendencies or desires to influence, resist, manipulate or control how the energy manifests.

We humans have grown (or should I say, atrophied) to distrust anything that's not tangible, physical, 3D phenomena... yet another demonstration of an addiction to limitation and polarity consciousness. But in doing so, we've grown to distrust the very source of our own all-knowing, subtle-yet-omnipotent selves that originate from beyond that comfort zone we've been defending.

But how can that be so when our conscious rational self (ego) also wants to be happy and fulfilled? Well, the ego believes it knows what will make us happy and becomes engrossed in pursuing whatever might uphold or confirm its existing beliefs.

Unfortunately, ego remains unaware that it's only working with crude information from the five basic senses and therefore choosing from only the limited menu of possibilities that are staring it in the face from the gross material world. It's not aware of the unlimited potentiality of the cosmic energy beyond our physical reality. It doesn't even know, or want to know, that it has created that limiting material world so is only looking at its self made boundaries believing they are absolute boundaries.

Ego has a weird and wondrous grip on human consciousness in this way. It perpetually limits your experience of life by inflicting its own narrow 3D perspective upon whatever newness you encounter or imagine might be possible.

Ego is like an animal tethered to a post: it can stand still or run as fast as it likes but it's always limited to circling the same post. If it wants its options to grow, it must find a way to let go and cut its ties to that familiar center of its world.

An effective way to unleash yourself is to deliberately alter your perspective on life. Instead of judging or evaluating new experiences from your existing point of view, try shifting your mindset over into the new circumstance for a moment. Then imagine looking back at your existing life from over there in the newness. Do your best to imagine that the new is already your norm. What would it be like to be happily in that new circumstance looking back? Re-evaluate yourself and your life from the standpoint of the new potential, being as honest and objective as you possibly can in the process.

When you open to channel more life force energy, the incoming frequencies are not familiar and more often than not disturb the usual you with strange sensations and ideas. To this, the ego silently says, "Hey what's that? It doesn't seem normal. I'd better avoid it or crush it so as not to endanger this predictable comfort zone and framework of truth I've created and am protecting." Bingo! Resistance to the energy.

As well, there are usually physical sensations as the energy runs through your body, to which the ego reacts, "This feels strange and unfamiliar," which it equates with uncomfortable and unpredictable. "Unfamiliar is bad and I don't want to feel it because I don't understand it and can't control it. I'll resist it, otherwise it might threaten the control I have over my world." Another block.

The mind also gets a hit, especially when it receives thoughts or ideas that don't validate the framework of believing on which the ego has been relying. "Hey, that's an idea. Maybe I could change my occupation and be happy living in a different place." So those ideas get squashed as well or relegated to the dungeons of suppression that are already cramming full of everything the ego considered unreal, incredible or unacceptable because it challenged the comfort zone. "Don't be stupid. You know you won't get the status and money and recognition in another line of work and, hey, you like this old place, anyway, at least you know where the problems are; and it's home, right? It's easier to stay; less hassles. Right?" Reacting in such a way, ego is denying your basic reason for being—to experience all that life has to offer—as well as, ironically, its own basic premise to find happiness and fulfillment *out there* as opposed to 'in here.'

The more you block the expression of life force energy, the more you're discovering what it's like to live a low frequency, fearful, diseased, pained, limited version of yourself.

There is no judgment on whatever you or anyone else chooses to experience in life, other than the judgmental aspersions that an ego casts upon it. Every experience is simply more learning; more data for the cosmic computer's data banks. Why then would you not choose to do more of the things that you'd love to do instead of things you feel obligated or forced to do? Why not choose joyous pastimes instead of unfulfilling ones? Why not fill your life with loving actions instead of hating or desperate ones? It's only a matter of choosing.

As far as the Supreme Mind is concerned, it makes absolutely no difference what any experience is so long as each individual's reality is unique. When it is, then the cosmos is expanding, exploring the unknown potentiality. Every experience then is cosmically perfect, ideal regardless of how it's judged by you or anyone else.

If two individuals were to have an identical experience, it would render one of them obsolete. Like a computer wasting space with duplicate files, the cosmos would waste its opportunity, its energy and its potentiality by unnecessary replication. But the cosmos is elegant and perfectly efficient; it wastes nothing.

Every person's individuality creates their unique experiences which are vital stitches in an infinite tapestry called 'The experience of physical life.' Its creative genius is the Supreme Mind—the Source of All That Is—and the cosmic artist is humankind. That's you and me.

Every moment in your life is a stroke of brilliance in the masterpiece. Each stroke is unique—another experience without which the picture would be incomplete. The Cosmic Intelligence relies on the principle 'Different strokes for different folks.'

Only egos go about trying to control other people's actions, beliefs and experiences, forcing or coercing them into sameness—to fit in with the status quo so that they won't contradict or challenge the predictable comfort zones of mass approval and acceptability. It's just one ego trying to get another's picture to match theirs, or trying to make theirs match another's, instead of allowing an entire array of masterpieces to emerge and create a rich and diverse gallery.

One's Higher Self doesn't act with such fear, control and judgment. It's an instrument of only joyous love—absolute allowance—and will therefore allow the fragile ego its wasteful and fearful games until you become fed up with its antics and open to real life with all its richness and vibrance.

That's the moment you move to a more direct connection with your Higher Self and begin consciously channeling the Divine energy for your own spiritual development and see it materialize throughout your life.

Every time you allow yourself to mould to the influence of your Higher Self, you more profoundly connect to its sweet nurturing whisper; the voice that exists for no other reason than to guide you on your unique path to absolute fulfillment.

THE MATTER OF ENERGY

When you're aligned with your Higher Self, you live your Inner Truth without compromise or hesitation. Because you've found the infinite power of your soul, you take full responsibility for creating every moment of your reality, and bathe in the magical, loving, abundant and spontaneous process that's life. In the process, via your Higher Self, you channel energies from higher dimensions of intelligence into our universe of human experience.

If you're not aligned with your Higher Self, you're still channeling but the energies are no longer direct from a higher source, they're personal and limited versions, disabled to the extent that you're living only a limited version of yourself for fear and ignorance of change, power and responsibility.

You're a cosmic translation device. When open and surrendered to higher consciousness you're tuned to receive energy being transmitted from realms which operate on an entirely different system of existence. You bring it in and translate it into your own personal system, then send the translation out into your reality as *you*—your personality, your truth, your actions... your life. The vital uniqueness of your personal translation is evident in the various physical, emotional and mental expressions of yourself in the world.

This translation process is like trying to read a book that's published in a foreign language. The author and the reader don't speak each other's language so a translator is needed. The final reader's understanding and appreciation of the author's original writing then becomes dependent upon how faithful the translation is to the original.

Any translation is governed by the translator's comprehension and appreciation of the original material, along with their literary ability, vocabulary and grammar. Whether they're objective about the material is also important since objectivity will tend to be more faithful, having no vested interest or agenda to satisfy. Accuracy, though, is easily compromised by any tendency to influence the original with personal biases, foibles, conditioning and present boundaries of acceptance.

Obviously, distortions can easily arise at any point through this translation process that you undertake in life. Because your prevailing state of awareness is not familiar with the incoming data, the translation you make is likely to be influenced by your present capabilities, beliefs, attitudes and conditioning. These influences filter the translation, flavoring it with the same limitations and biases that your ego creates, reinforces and defends.

The incoming consciousness first enters as purely conceptual information—an unconscious idea that's 'dropped into' your own stream of consciousness like flower petals cast onto a river. It immediately begins translating into images, feelings, thoughts or words that your awareness can identify at the time. It's like recognizing a flower petal or two later on the river downstream. Even if the mind cannot exactly translate the data, it's all that's available at the time.

Numerous times whilst channeling a higher energy,

I've experienced the sensation of that incoming intelligence hunting around in my mind looking for words to describe some vast or cosmic principle it wants to convey.

The accuracy and effectiveness of your unique translation into life depends upon your particular type of personal operating system—the way that you *be you* and *do* life. Are you in allowance or resistance, clear or blocked, flexible or biased? Are you defending some comfort zone or familiar mindset?

At this point begins your filtering which influences the energy. This, too, happens according to your own personality. Take the vocal example: all vocal communication uses sounds which are made in a particular way, connected into sequences and groups that create words and phrases that people mutually recognize and understand. That's speech.

The new life force energy you allow in through your channel might translate into ideas with which you're not familiar, requiring words or phrases that are unfamiliar as well. The instant these begin to form in the mind, the rational, limitation-addicted mental structure steps forward and tells you, "This is unrecognizable. You must be making it up. It's just rubbish; it doesn't make sense," and pulls the plug on your channeling experience by convincing you it's a waste of time.

Alternatively, you may find that the words and phrases are indeed familiar to you, in which case the rational mind says, "You were going to explore something new and different, but I know this stuff so it must be just you making it up" and pulls the plug just the same. For this reason it's vital to ignore the ego's intervention into channeling and to allow the flow to happen effortlessly.

In whatever way you experience the incoming energy, the ego initially reacts in some way to pull you back to your conditioning and familiarity with limiting beliefs about yourself and your world. It finds all manner of reasons and ways to block the flow because you're becoming conscious of things that disturb the status quo and challenge the validity of your comfort zone.

It's very easy for it to undermine your advancement since the whole process of channeling the new energies is happening in the heart center through self trust, a quality with which many people are not very familiar.

Once the flow of new energy starts, it takes self discipline to allow the cosmic life force to continue without interfering with it, compromising its purity and lowering its original frequency.

But then, discipline is what disciples are made of, and the disciples of all great spiritual masters were not devoted to their master but to what that master stood for—devotion to the use and maintenance of their own unique channel; devotion to their own connection to God and Supreme wisdom, their Higher Self and their own divinity. They were disciplined in their constant attention to and refinement of that channel. The master they followed was simply an exemplary guide to that discipline. The disciples adhered to the discipline, following the example, not the person.

Any true spiritual master has never asked people to follow and depend upon them, though sadly it's most often the result. Their discipline and service was to constantly encourage and assist their disciples or devotees to be *in*-dependent, self responsible and self realized creators of life with full awareness of that power. The master didn't want them to be dependent and master-realized or guru-realized and they certainly didn't need to realize the divinity of the disciples— the *disciples* needed to real-ize (make real) their own divinity themselves.

Self realization and enlightenment obviously requires a far greater amount of trust (faith in self and the process), love, courage, insight and discipline than is required to realize the divinity of someone else who is already demonstrating it openly.

When self realized, one expresses into the world their own Inner Truth. As they do, it becomes more and more purely an expression of the higher life force energy that pours through them in their actions, their attitudes and their words, regardless of the prevailing beliefs and conditions that may surround them.

For any vocal channel, the most basic of all hurdles is the sound of their own voice. It's common for people to feel embarrassed or self conscious when their own voice is recorded and played back. Likewise, when channeling verbally, the rational mind hears that familiar sound, regardless of the words being spoken, and immediately tells you, "You said you were going to let someone new and different and more enlightened communicate, but this is just you. You're making this up" and pulls the plug yet again.

This could begin to look like a hopeless task but

find confidence in the fact that the Higher Intelligence communicates by pure telepathy—instantaneous thought transfer—not by words. Words require sound which is lower frequency energy than intelligence of higher realms can manage. They use us for that! For them, communicating by words would be about as feasible and practical as us trying to communicate an encyclopedia of information to a chicken by trying to squawk and squeak like one.

Voice communication is only for creatures living in a 3D space-time environment. Sound will not travel through a vacuum. That's why to create soundproofing you must construct a sealed airless space between two surfaces such as sheets of glass. Any sound that manages to get through the first layer of glass is lost in the space between and never gets past the second layer.

The point is that sound requires a carrier substance such as air or water to enable the sound waves to form and travel. That substance occupies space. Also, for those waves to travel from their transmitter to a receiver requires time. So there we are, living in our space-time world, speaking to and hearing from each other, all the while mistakenly believing it's the only means of communication possible.

Telepathy, on the other hand, is non physical, unfiltered, flawless and instantaneous thought transfer. It's only compromised by the quality of the receiver.

That's how the realms of higher intelligence communicate with us. They place a thought into the flow of consciousness entering us as life force energy (again, like casting the petals on the river).

It then becomes part of our consciousness; either an unconscious part or, hopefully, a conscious part of which we're aware. We receive it and, if we're conscious of it, our challenge and discipline is to do our utmost not to distort or degrade it as we transmit it into our reality in human terms.

The slightest interference by our personality foibles compromises the cosmic wisdom that beings of Supreme intelligence have endeavored to transfer to us for our enlightenment, evolution and the Highest Good.

If you've ever said something unfamiliar yet profound or erudite in a particularly relaxed, lucid or important moment that has given you the thought "Where did that come from?" then you'll know what it is to spontaneous link cosmic telepathy to your regular speech function without interference. That's a sign of practical everyday channeling and indicates that you're 'in touch' and functioning as a conduit for higher intelligence.

In addition to direct voice channeling, there are countless other forms channeling takes. Life itself is the process of channeling the cosmic life force energy. The actual form it takes depends on your personal free will.

Just like your life in every passing moment, all forms of channeling are subject to the same compromising ego influences as the direct voice channeling of the cosmic masters.

Any overt creative activity such as music, art, writing, healing, spiritual counseling, singing, inventing, dancing, even plain old relaxed conversation are all channeling more directly than any activity in which you *try* to channel.

You can only *allow* channeling to take place, you can't make it happen. It's spontaneous and open to other people's judgment and interpretation and this vulnerability challenges ego judgment and conditioning more intensely in the person channeling. It therefore presents the greatest healing opportunity for them to overcome their resistance to allowing the channeled energy's unbridled flow.

In all instances it's a matter of how far the limited you (that uses all the conditioning and biases) can stand back and stop interfering with the *un*limited you that's like an innocent child attempting to blossom forth in service to your own self realization, power and fulfillment.

All of the blocks the limited self puts in the way represent self doubt and self denial. Self denial is the opposite of self allowance, or self love. Every time you suppress or deny the validity of your uniqueness and natural power to create, enabling your limitations, biases and conditioning to influence you in any way, you're lowering your own consciousness vibration.

On the other hand, every time you trust your inner impulses you positively affect the way your life manifests before your eyes.

ACCELERATED MANIFESTATION

Try pressing the palms of your hands together—hard! It doesn't matter how much pressure you exert they go nowhere and you achieve little more than exhausting your energy. That's the way resistance and conflict work, energetically speaking. When there are conflicting intentions and thought forms, there is no clear message to the Creation Force and nothing gets created exactly the way you want it.

Every person has the same inherent Divine power and right to manifest whatever they choose in their life just by the discipline of focusing their thoughts, attention, emotions and actions. As Henry Ford said: "Whether you think you can or think you can't, you're right."

The only time it doesn't work is when one set of thoughts conflicts with another set. This can happen when you're doing something that contributes to the manifestation whilst thinking something that undermines or contradicts it. For example, saying "I'll work hard to save a million dollars" and working every God given hour whilst thinking "I wish I didn't have to work so hard; I know I'll never have a million dollars." Your mental energy is confused as well as being in conflict with the physical energy. The result is that the power of both is cancelled out by the conflict. The result—no million dollars.

A similar effect is achieved when one person tries to create something opposite to someone else's wishes, or they try to change another's way of thinking, forcing them to be a part of something that's not their deepest wishes or for their highest good. In such instances, the Creation Force is again cancelled out by the two competing thought forms and nobody gets satisfaction.

This happens in relationships where one of the partners has one agenda while the other has a different, even opposing plan. One might want a holiday abroad while the other wants a quiet time at home. Ego consciousness encourages one of the two partners to become stronger, more determined or overpowering than the other in order to achieve their preference. After all, there has to be a winner and a loser in ego's polarity mindset. But as one wins their way, the other has suppressed or denied their own dream. The outcome is that the relationship has a conflict in it and is set up to drain its energy into the futility of conflict instead of into empowering some mutual creation. But why not do both?

Competition of any kind yields no winner, in truth. It only wastes energy that could have been used fruitfully in cooperation and co-creation of a common goal.

The world over, humankind suffers immeasurably under this principle, constantly depleting an invaluable supply of creative energy. When masses of people agree to create something in unison, it will change the world effortlessly and almost instantaneously.

When a person's will is to create something for themselves whilst remaining detached about the exact form it might take or about how others might be affected by it, the thought forms have a far greater chance to materialize more quickly and accurately. Moreover, when those thought images are translated into sound, carried into the world by voice and speech, their potential to manifest is accelerated still more.

It will always serve you well to listen to what you're saying each moment of each day and to express only words that describe what you wish your life to be or what you want to create in your life. Alternatively, describe what you love about your life at present.

Avoid discussing what upsets or disappoints you or others. Discuss your loves, dreams and aspirations instead, no matter what others may think of them. *"Great minds discuss ideas; average minds discuss events; small minds discuss people."* (Eleanor Roosevelt).

Sound, being a relatively low set of frequencies on the spectrum of electromagnetic energy, is a very *physical* energy. It vibrates your eardrums so you can hear; it moves substances as it makes waves; it can crack crystal and induce physical nausea, even death when transmitted in certain frequencies. "In the beginning was the word and the word was God" translates as "In the beginning of material creation was sound and the sound was the resonance of Om." The Om represents the vibration of the life force energy that first participates in our dense material realm.

Because of this power that is inherent in sound, all that you speak about is more likely to manifest than what you don't speak about. Even what you say in jest, abhorrence or fear is harnessed by this powerful Creation Force and faithfully brought closer to material form. This is the Cosmic Law of Creation further empowered. It's absolutely infallible and inevitable.

Problems have arisen as humans have forgotten and ignored this fundamental cosmic principle. Instead they've tried to find some reason other than themselves for their insufferable predicaments. Over vast time, ignorance of our power to create our lives became more ingrained while knowledge of that power dissipated. Instead ignorance, victim mentality and blame became the normal view of life, and personal powerlessness accepted as an inevitable fact of life.

Understandably, caught up in such a thoroughly convincing ocean of disempowerment, people lost any will or reason to discipline their thoughts and attitudes and communication. After all, what difference could it make? Unfortunately, they had no idea there was such a powerful gift at their fingertips.

As time, generations and lifetimes passed, even their will and purpose to generate their own thoughts and ideals waned in favor of the ones given them by family, religion, education, government, economy, creed and culture—outside influences. People's ability to think for themselves atrophied; it was easier to accept the beliefs, ideas, attitudes and thoughts of outside sources, regardless of their underlying motives. At least if something went wrong there was someone else to blame (...wasn't there?). They were just another set of beliefs anyway (...weren't they?).

But of course each of those acquired mindsets was a creation seed. Not only that, it was initiated by a person, group, system or culture almost certainly self interested, having little concern for preserving a person's uniqueness or highest good, instead wanting to preserve their own power, control or benefit.

These were rules developed by egos and their systems to indoctrinate, control and homogenize people rather than to enlighten, liberate and empower them. Mass belief systems bore little or no resemblance to any individual's deepest desires and aspirations; certainly no accordance with their *highest* good, self realization or emergence into personal power.

Now, however, having read these pages you're aware of this Cosmic Law and have a choice. Will you start generating a reality under your jurisdiction or will you continue to squirm around in the consensus reality under the influence of some outside power?

Now that you have the awareness of this basic Cosmic Law, you have power in every single moment of your own life. You can take the responsibility and discipline to honor your God given power as a creator "born in the image of the Creator"; to use that power and spiritual responsibility to begin manifesting whatever *you* consider your highest ideals for yourself and your own life by harboring only the thoughts and speaking only about what's most deeply desirable to *you*.

Alternatively, you can choose to ignore it and continue through life as a victim of outside influences and conditions, blaming for your predicaments anything but the real source—yourself—and continuing to feel powerless and unfulfilled.

If that's the case, then with this awareness, you can't offset the blame for any circumstance without lying to yourself and to the Divine. Sometime, somehow for some reason, you chose it by *allowing* it to occupy your conscious thoughts and feelings instead of choosing to dwell on something else more desirable.

Studying the choices you've made 'sometime, somehow for some reason' is valuable self inquiry and is a part of your path to enlightenment. Taking responsibility for having created everything in your life launches you as the architect of your future, not a victim of it. Initially, the rational preconditioned mind says "Oh, but even when I change my thoughts, the change doesn't materialize".

One reason is that it takes time, consistent thought and focus, exactly as it did to materialize your present circumstances. The delay is only temporary and, like anything, practice makes perfect. Nobody learns to ride a bicycle skillfully at the first attempt. Remember, you're used to dealing with lower frequency energy which takes considerably longer to manifest; it couldn't flow in and reshape to fill your 'thought mould' as quickly as lighter, higher frequency energy can. Patience and continual discipline are vital to replace old habits and patterns with new ones.

Another reason for the time lapse in creation is that the human mind still has thousands of thoughts of unwanted stuff. When you introduce new desirable thoughts, they are usually a minority so get a minority of the attention and a relative amount of creation energy. That is, at least, until you've disciplined yourself to give them more and more attention than the old ones.

Some of what you're experiencing in your present

reality is the result of thoughts and mindsets you favored days, months, years, decades and lifetimes ago. Little wonder you don't recall having the thoughts! And little wonder many people consider karma a punishment from some exotic force that seems to 'do it to them.' You've gone through death and rebirth—a very effective filter—in order to be in a physical body and experience a physical reality with little or no long term awareness. Unless you're aware of the process brought about by the Cosmic Law of Creation and remember that it's molding every moment of your life, you'll not readily be able to see through the spiritual amnesia barrier that separates your lifetimes.

A major problem with forgetting that you'd held the thoughts in a previous incarnation or an earlier time in life is that when they do eventually materialize in your life, you think it was caused by some influence or power other than yourself. There's no obvious connection that you're aware of. That's how victim mentality has developed in an otherwise Supremely empowered species called humankind. It's all because we forgot—our power, our spiritual responsibilities, and the significance of our moment to moment thought patterns, beliefs and mindset.

To heal that broken connection, all you need do is perpetually remind yourself that you must have focused at some time on something or things that enabled this to manifest. Blame or retribution should not become the issue here, only acknowledging the connectedness and your responsibility as the creator.

In our present day and age, the frequency of the ambient energy—the ocean of consciousness in which we all exist in this world—has risen considerably and everyone is now able to tap into new higher frequencies of the life force energy if they so choose. These new frequencies will enable thoughts to materialize much more quickly—in seconds, minutes, hours or days—so that you can recognize them as actually having come from you rather than assuming they'd come from some other source as you'd previously been convinced by the time lapse and spiritual amnesia.

So how do you tap into these new higher frequency energies instead of continuing to work with old low frequency ones? Simple. Open to life. Go with the spontaneous flow of life, not against or across it. Continue to do only what happens relatively easily and naturally. If a direction or action becomes blocked or requires an inordinate amount of pressure or effort to overcome barriers then stop for a moment; if you're truly going with the flow you'll not need to force anything. Recognize when there are barriers or blocks in your path and take it as a sign to alter your direction in some way.

Only then can the potency of higher frequency energy enter your life. When it begins coursing through you, that wonderful—and sometimes perturbing—phenomenon arises where your thoughts and words begin to materialize in your physical reality much more quickly and accurately.

You begin to see, to realize, your own creation power and responsibility and are able to start doing something about any undesirable effects it may have in your life because you'll know you are actually in charge... the creator. That is to say, you begin to heal.

Refine your creation power by looking at every single existing circumstance in your life and saying to yourself "Look at that; I created that and now I know how. What do I need to adjust now in my own thoughts and beliefs to create something else in its place?" Then make the adjustments immediately and diligently. Apply that to everything, no exceptions; everything you like as well as everything you dislike.

In this new energy of life, every image and belief you have of your self, of your potential, and of the potential of your life will be made manifest for you to observe, evaluate and reassess so that you can choose to either hold onto it or to change it if it doesn't shape up to your evolving ideals.

Do remember however that the Creation Force looks into your mind like watching a TV screen, a screen that has no words or sound, only pictures—your mental pictures; your thought forms. The power of creation doesn't hear "want" or "don't want", "good" or "bad", "right" or "wrong", it just looks at your thought form—whatever you're thinking about or focusing on in your mind—and empowers it to materialize.

The Creation Force looks at images, it doesn't listen to words. Therefore whatever you want must be able to be made into a picture of some sort. 'Good' or 'wrong' can't form a picture because they're judgments whereas 'complicated' or 'happy' or 'small' are just observations and they can form in pictures.

Creation assumes that you're self loving enough to hold in your mind images only of what you'd love to experience, and it dedicates its energy to fulfilling your idea of life on that basis. Your spiritual task is to learn that and live by it unwaveringly to intentionally gain self awareness.

Take careful and clear note that *all* of your thought forms will be empowered to manifest, not just the ones you judge to be good, right or desirable. *All* of them will more rapidly and clearly become a reality for you. That means any of your negativities, biases or conditioning will become more abundantly clear to you than ever before. So will your allowance and love, for that matter. So if you continue to think you don't have enough of something then, sure enough, you'll keep materializing a lack of it. *Speak* about not having it and even more graphically you'll not have it in your life!

Instead, dream... regularly ignore the outer reality and put your energy and time and focus into what you most deeply wish so more of that will manifest. When you talk, continually talk about what you'd love in your life and ideas that exhilarate and excite you, instead of about problems or negativities that seem to exist or might happen.

Deal immediately with any negative circumstances or problems in your life on a practical level, but don't dwell on them, don't talk about them excessively and don't become preoccupied by them. Let go of them.

Having the idea that things are always the same will ensure that they stay that way. Start allowing yourself to have the attitude and belief that things are always getting better, and then look for the evidence in your life; it will be there. Instead of resisting change for fear of it bringing something worse, begin assuming that all change will bring only benefits, then so it will, more and more.

Finally, always give appreciation for things materializing. Thank yourself for having had the self love and focus, then thank the Creation Force itself for bringing you the energy and opportunity for that wonderful, accurate manifestation.

Creating a new reality is just a case of changing your mind about yourself, about your potential and about the potential of your life, and about all others and their potential. It's a brutally simple but infinitely powerful mind shift, and only you can make it on your behalf. If you think it's not worth the effort then that's fine, but remember that whatever you put out into your life in tangible physical actions or in more subtle emotional and mental actions *will* become very real for you regardless of whether or not you want it to or believe it will or like it.

As with any power you use, be it horsepower in a car, electrical power in your home or the cosmic power in your life, it's up to you to use it with care and responsibility to energize the things you truly want. If you flicked a light switch in your home and the electric oven came on instead of the radio, it would be confusing and frustrating, not to mention senseless. So instead of the electricity running appliances randomly in the house, we make sure that the power is guided to the things we *want* to work for us at the time. It's the same with creation. It's all energy management.

Life force energy doesn't actually care what it empowers to materialize in your life because it doesn't judge. It relies on you to manage it by way of your mind and faithfully empowers whatever thought picture is presented to it, intentionally or unintentionally, on your mental TV screen.

The more you open to life, the more you'll receive the power of the higher energies and the faster your thoughts will materialize. Even more you'll need to remember that where your attention goes, energy flows.

As we grow beyond the ignorance with which we've abused this gift in the past, we all have an inescapable spiritual responsibility to direct the creation power ourselves deliberately and with appreciation of its inescapable force, of our own inescapable potency, and of the vital requirement for energy management through self discipline.

POWER ON

To harness the Creation Force in your life, your attention will first need to be given to the discipline of *Self Watching*. This does not mean self criticism—beating yourself up is of no use at all to you nor to the cosmos. *Self Watching* means taking a long, hard look at yourself and the way you're *being* in your life at every moment. Being self aware is the result.

Self Watching requires being one hundred percent honest with yourself about your mindset, your thoughts and attitudes, your communication and your intention behind everything you do, or don't do, in every single moment. It involves becoming ever more aware of what your mind and attention is on. In any instance, is that really your deepest wish, or is not? Do you really want to be in conflict or would you rather be at peace? Does your attitude really resemble what you want more of in life, or not? Are you acting with love or control? Honestly. Does that belief you hold to so dearly really work in bringing you more fulfillment or does it require an unreasonable amount of effort to enforce? Are you following your deepest wishes or the influence of the 'should' and 'ought to' conditioning?

The discipline of *Self-Watching* is necessary because if more of your time and thought is directed at what you *don't* want or *don't* like, then you're going to get exactly that—what you don't want—and it's entirely your own doing.

Remember: your thought forms do not carry the preference you have, only your image, idea or thought picture of the thing or circumstance. If you often think about not wanting to be poor or hungry, your inner imaging system that's focusing the energy for manifestation will faithfully see the thought form of poverty and hunger. It'll be completely oblivious to your attitudes *about* it, such as 'want' or 'don't want,' good or bad, right or wrong. And... congratulations! You'll create for yourself poverty and hunger.

Instead, though, having now watched yourself think that way, begin to reconstruct your thinking; discipline your thoughts to focus on what you *do* want—perpetually, relentlessly, uncompromisingly.

Always think about abundance and wellbeing and develop a sense that they're more and more present as each moment passes. They will then begin to manifest more and more. While you're at it, remember to think it's easy and quick, not difficult and slow, so that you don't manifest a strugglesome process of achieving your aims.

The most immediate and effective way to become in tune with and knowing of the universe's view of your creation requests is to totally quit judging anything, anyone, any time for any reason anywhere in your life—perpetually, uncompromisingly, relentlessly. No more good/ bad, right/ wrong, should/ shouldn't or better/ worse. Then and only then will you benefit from seeing your life the way the Supreme Intelligence sees it. Think that's a tall order? Then try changing its material effects in your life! It's far easier to re-form thought than matter.

Criticism is the venom of the ego. It's a form of judgment and as such is based on judgment's arbitrary set of preferences. Those preferences were inherited during childhood innocence but they've become seemingly concrete over years of reinforcing them, justifying them and fighting for them.

Be aware of when you're judging anything and instead ask yourself what you *really* think about it. What rational, accurate observation can you make that you are willing to claim as yours personally?

To just say something is wrong contributes nothing but resistance and conflict. Think first about what you honestly mean and take personal responsibility for it. You might find that you say "I don't like it" or "I don't agree with it." You might say "It appears to hurt people unnecessarily" or "I think there is another way to look at it that's just as valid." Any of these expresses your personal viewpoint, invites discussion and allows others to agree or disagree.

Acknowledge that others have their own view, just as valid as yours, and make space for it to be expressed instead of shutting it out. At least you'll give yourself the opportunity to stop and become aware of yourself, then find out what your real truth is.

Consciously rebuilding thought patterns in such a way is the second discipline, *Mind Shifting*. By this discipline, you allow yourself to change your mind about yourself and your life. You remember to alter your mindset whenever you see an opportunity in life to do so, as long as it's going to support a more expansive, joyous and fulfilled you and a self image of power and dominion throughout your life, not one of weakness, fear or victimhood.

Always be flexible enough in your beliefs and

attitudes to shift your mindset in order to see yourself and your life in a fresh and supportive light, no matter how you see it right now. As I mentioned previously, the system has always worked in this way, you just didn't realize it. Your life, your reality and your experiences outside have always been a perfect and clear reflection of who you were choosing to be inside.

Whatever fears, biases, attitudes, controls and conditioning that you've chosen to hold onto, as well as whatever love, allowance, flexibility and creativity you've been choosing to embrace in your life, result in what your life looks like at this moment, right now.

Having learned this, certainly you can no longer blame anyone else for your predicaments. More importantly, neither need you thank anyone else for your successes as many tend to do and thereby give away their self power in yet another form. It's all you— you have always had the power and always will.

Furthermore, don't concern yourself with what others might think of the new you or your new attitudes. Elbert Hubbard said "To avoid criticism... do nothing, say nothing, be nothing!" Copernicus was the only one who believed that the planets revolved around the Sun, not around the Earth, and everyone at the time thought he was crazy, threatening to kill him for insisting on such anti-God lies.

That indicates the level of flexibility and sanity of status quo belief systems. The mass mindset is not the correct mindset, only the usual or popular one. In its longing to blame and judge others, it betrays its epidemic fear of having true personal power. Why? Because with personal power comes true personal responsibility for it's use, an unmistakable bomb under the ego's age old and dilapidated safe house called Blame.

The responsibility of personal power automatically begins to discipline not only a person's attitudes but their actions as well.

Which brings me to the third discipline, *Honest Action*—acting upon your words and thoughts with true integrity, even in the face of potential adversity or conflict. If you find you can't do this, then you'd better reconsider your personal truth. Do you truly believe now what you were taught as a child at school or by your parents? Do you deeply resonate with what your government or religion asks you to believe? Do they foster in you an understanding of your self power and sovereignty throughout your life? Do they strengthen your self esteem and sense of worthiness, capability and independence? Do they support an image of your life being increasingly one of love and joy, peace and abundance and fulfillment?

The discipline of *Honest Action* becomes progressively more simple because when you say one thing and do another, it's very obvious to all and sundry. Along with the rest of your world, you become more conscious of your actions and of any discrepancies between them and your Inner Truth. You'll become less able to ignore any instances where you're not living by your truth but living a lie instead. Along with you, other people will notice if you were, for example, to say in conversation "I think generosity is important" or "I believe in peace" then act in a miserly or aggressive way in your day-to-day circumstances. Where would be your sincerity in that?

Look at our world and imagine your were a being from a distant star system, had studied the human species and their behavior and way of life in detail. Now you want to make contact. You land on Earth and the first thing the frightened humans say is that they want you to come in peace, friendship and good will. Knowing the history of the human race, you'd need to have a sense of humor...

You're aware now that you're completely responsible for your entire reality as it is, like it or not. But you can also change your Now reality since you're the only one with absolute command over it—over your life and your experiences.

That's your true responsibility and power, and when you're aware of and utilize that power in every moment of your life with absolute responsibility, you're living more of your divinity and getting closer and closer to your life purpose—your reason for being on the planet.

As you open to life force energy and allow it to flow unhindered through your channels and apply to it the disciplines of *Self Watching*, *Mind Shifting* and *Honest Action*, your life will begin to transform as sublime qualities manifest throughout it—abundance, a deep sense of purpose, peace, unconditional love, service to humanity and Mother Earth, joy, ease and fulfillment to name just a few.

The very process you'll have undertaken and committed to action will continually add power and speed to your own healing by reinforcing your connection to your Higher Self and manifesting your spirituality throughout everyday life.

ACCELERATED HEALING

Think for a moment. Do you have any resistances to or doubts concerning your unbridled expression and the acceptance of your own perfection and divinity? If your answer is yes, or if you even hesitated, those are blocks to the pure life force energy. Those blocks didn't form overnight. They have built up over lifetimes, years and generations, through cultures and civilizations. Many are ancient and very deep seated; some more recent ones may be relatively superficial. Nevertheless, they have all taken some time to densify the energy in your consciousness, and they'll most likely take more than a moment or two to dissolve again, or heal.

Imagine that the free flowing energy in the higher realms were water that has now densified into ice due to resistances to its flow of warmth and love. Expose that ice to hot water and you'll obviously melt it back to a free flowing liquid state again.

That's exactly how channeled cosmic life force energy works in healing. Anyone who allows the higher interdimensional energies through their being with little or no resistance is allowing their entire energy system, physical and non physical, to be exposed to the intensity of that energy. By sheer exposure to the higher frequencies, any energy that has become congested and forms disease will be melted down like hot water melting ice. With no more densified energy there's no longer any threat of dis-ease.

That doesn't mean that it fixes everything for

you, but it does offer the raw materials required to rebuild a dis-eased body into one of perfect form and function. That is, of course, if you're prepared to allow your biases and conditioning to dissolve permanently as you come into alignment with your changes in consciousness.

For example, if your conditioning tells you not to speak your mind because you might upset someone, then when you begin channeling the cosmic life force energies you'll most likely find yourself attracting that very situation to you in all sorts of ways—being asked your opinion or invited to speak publicly; having to speak up in support of yourself; finding yourself in an intimate situation requiring your inner most feelings to be communicated; or even to perform a counseling function. It's because that self limiting belief requires healing if you're to dissolve the dis-ease that would otherwise be its result.

Your discipline is to be aware of yourself and your life circumstances (*Self Watching*), not as a victim but as a master seeing every circumstance as Divine guidance (*Mind Shifting*) and to say to yourself, "Here's that situation again. I've obviously created it once more so there is undoubtedly something I've still not learned yet. I now have a choice: I can react fearfully by compromising my communication and stifling my truth again, or I can respond with love by honoring my unique self and allowing my own truth to flow with compassion and composure, without emotional conditioning, judgment, aggression or control attached."

Choosing the latter (*Honest Action*) will inevitably bring some awkward situations and emotions to the fore. But that isn't bad nor wrong, just unfamiliar and uncomfortable. They're all just signs of things you'd pushed back into the dungeons of suppression, things that are now released and flowing through and out of your energy field. This is the process of your unconscious becoming conscious; the unseen causes of disease becoming known to you so that you can dissolve and heal them.

If you can't feel it, you can't heal it. The physical human body feels sensations only when energy is moving through it. The uncomfortable situations are simply stifled emotional energy becoming available to your healing process so it can be transmuted back into higher frequency form that's of benefit to you rather than hindrance.

This outward flow of suppressed energy might manifest as tears or laughter, hot flushes or perspiration, or for that matter any other form that might be typical—argumentativeness, anger, solitude, creative activity or physical exertion to name a few.

But that's how we heal once and for all—by feeling the feelings, identifying and being at peace with them, and willing ourselves to rethink and re-express them in healthy ways that produce peace and release, or bring us closer to joy and fulfillment instead of more of the same old stuff.

Open to life and allow yourself to become exposed to all manner of circumstances. Revel in your vulnerability and it will bring out all manner of feelings so you can learn to handle it differently, using your life experiences to grow and evolve as was always intended. There is nothing wrong with the feelings, they're just Supreme Will pointing out how different it is to your ego's will.

So let it go. Just will yourself to let go of the conflict and forget it. Simple. Though it can take enormous courage and strength at the time, you'll achieve better health on all levels and develop higher consciousness as a result. No one can do this for you; it's your spiritual path and responsibility, ready and waiting for the moment you allow yourself to grasp it and heal.

EXPERIENCING ENERGY

One of the major issues to contend with for someone opening their own channels to a greater influx of higher frequency Light (life force energy) is that of *Experiential Energy*—the actual feelings and sensations that a person experiences at the time as an immediate and direct result of allowing a vastly intensified stream of the energy to pour into and through them.

These sensations are strongest at the first contact with the energy, after which much of the intensity normally subsides as the person's blocks are flooded and their energy system assimilates the new intensity and adapts automatically.

My Cosmic Activation workshop (in a slightly different and elementary format, its was previously called Opening to Channel) is a truly experiential one. In it I facilitate the preparation, clearing and opening of people's own direct channel to the life force energy. The connection takes place at a highly spiritual level through self allowance and meditation techniques with me providing only the opportunity, the energetic environment and the appropriate tools and methodology.

For a decade, the world over I've run this workshop and on every occasion it's unique, taking place in different ways according to the individuals attending. Many remarkable things transpire as each person has exactly the experiences that suit their own unique path of growth, expansion and healing at the time.

Consistently I've found that in each group, most

of those attending have similar experiences to each other in addition to their own unique ones. These can include the release of some long standing family issue, a decision to change job or eating habits, a realization of deep appreciation of someone, a commitment to some service, or something else of which the person had previously been unaware or disinclined towards. I see this as a sign of mutual threads of connection on a higher, spiritual, non rational level.

Even though many people at a single event have never met before, they nevertheless seem to have come together in the workshop to share something additional to the actual activation. Whatever that something is, it's what determines the shared experiences they have, aside from their own individual ones.

Similarly, in group meditation and channeling events where many individuals are gathered for only a couple of hours, during the sharing that follows, people often mention that the channeled transmission has been deeply meaningful to them personally. They insist that it has related to their exact life circumstances at the time or simply resonated within them as a deep truth, on a level they'd not previously felt and often can't explain. But the really curious thing is that often more than half those attending share the same sentiment after the same event.

How can a limited number of words be so specifically meaningful to so many people at one time? Hardly coincidence when it happens so consistently. The *energy* upon which the channeled words are conveyed achieves that remarkable feat, enabling everyone present to get from the transmission whatever was meant for them individually. I for one cannot begin to imagine how that could be achieved if anyone actually set their mind to achieving. It happens by simply allowing it to take place, understanding that it can and trusting that it will.

The difference between channeling just words and channeling energy-with-words is that energy is able to convey qualities such as alliance, kinship, love, compassion or understanding that a rational mind could never do. The synergy of the energy and words create not only speech to fascinate the rational mind but also a force to nourish and stimulate the spirit, emotions and body in myriad unfathomable ways.

All such phenomena, mutual as well as individual, are *Experiential Energy* manifesting as mental, emotional or physical occurrences.

Mentally, it often takes the form of confusion, simply because the actual energy sensations a person experiences at the time conflict with their existing set of beliefs and understandings about what was true and possible. This can be intensified by the awareness that it is undeniably they themselves who are actually experiencing it, not someone else whom they could refute more easily. Since it's actually happening to them personally, they can't seriously deny its existence. Worry or stress can also arise since they don't rationally know what they're experiencing, how to deal with it or how to control it. Sheer wonder at the new and remarkable sensations they're having can flood their minds; even outright disbelief that it could actually be happening.

Emotionally, a person can feel upset and weepy or enlivened and giggly, regretful and guilty or confident and excited, or enthused or disturbed. This is often a response to a sudden influx of unconscious present and past life memories which are stored deeply and have not been resolved or released. It can also be latent suppressed emotional issues being released for balancing and healing.

Physically, people often feel unusual sensations running through their body; hot or cold flushes, or both; physically shaking or becoming weak and unable to move; aches and pains which appear and disappear during the event; vibrations in their spine and back; muscle spasms; itching or tingling on the skin; excessive perspiration; a runny nose or eyes; even toothache.

These phenomena are signs of the physical form of the person adapting to a higher state of energy by releasing blocks in those ways. This adaptation requires that their body's dense materialized energy allows adjustments to take place in its lower consciousness portions. Disease, for instance, that had been formed or is in the process of forming must let go of its old density to which it has become accustomed so that the new higher vibrations can be allowed in.

Those few examples simply illustrate the way people's individual state of consciousness—the present status of their unique combination of mental, emotional and physical energy—experiences, translates and adapts to the new vibrations and intensities of Light and the new consciousness it brings.

Surely it makes perfect sense that when you invite in greater life force, neither you nor your life can remain the same. Like pouring hot water into a bowl of ice water, the original receptacle and its contents are no longer the same in many ways and for many reasons. When you open to life in such a direct way by connecting more closely to the source, you'll not remain the same—you'll begin to experience yourself and your life as you never had before.

Just like adapting to a different climate, so must you adjust to the new energy flow. Only when the adjustment has been made will you feel comfortable with it and able to integrate it more easily throughout your life.

If you don't consciously and diligently go about making the adjustment then the connection procedure becomes just another fleeting experience and you'll naturally revert to the old arrangement of life and convince yourself that the connection was a waste of time. Like going to a hot place from a cold one, your metabolism adapts to the new climate but if you decide to return to the cold, so does it revert easily to its old ways.

The adjustment process asks that a person train themselves to stay connected to the energy perpetually, in every moment diligently applying *Self Watching*, *Mind Shifting* and *Honest Action*; constantly reviewing their attitudes, beliefs, actions and reactions in life with the intention to release the old consciousness and integrate the new without resisting it. After all, opening to life is intended to bring the opportunity to change your life in positive, uplifting and fulfilling ways, and it does.

In doing so, only you can exercise the courage, strength and discipline to make a difference whenever you have the opportunity; that is to say, whenever a change in experience, feeling, understanding or attitude conflicts with your ego's desire to retain or defend your old personal comfort zone. Opportunities will continue to arise where you can make a profound difference, and nobody but you can make the choice at that moment to flow with the new and let the old dissolve away.

Having diligently made adjustments to the new energies, there comes a point where many people believe the energy has gone away—they don't feel the sensations any more and they believe they still need them in order to confirm the continuing presence of the new energy. This is actually a sign that they have indeed adjusted and healed to some extent; some of their emotional, physical and mental debris has been dissolved from their channels allowing the energy to flow freely without obstructions.

Sensations are really a sign of blockages, so when blockages have been dissolved there'll be no sensations; the energy will flow easily and naturally without physical effects or dramatic sensations.

Some people think that the sensations they feel from the incoming new energy are actually some evil force present or attacking them. Others believe it's 'bad energy', or even negative entities or destructive harmful beings interfering from some other plane of existence. Because they're initially not at ease with the unusually heightened energy, these people feel ill at ease with it and this message of dis-ease gets sent to this thinking mind. The thinking mind sifts through its existing knowledge stores and says it must be something bad because it's unknown and it's upsetting the usual equilibrium.

What's actually happened is the person's energetic comfort zone has been shaken up and their ego doesn't like it. The ego is used to going into its personal encyclopedia of fears and victimhood beliefs and dragging out anything it can find to convince you to discontinue any unfamiliar or disturbing activity for no other reason than it being disruptive or uncomfortable.

Based on the cosmic principle of karma whereby you'll experience the manifestation of your own strongest thought forms, a person can easily manifest all sorts of ghosties and googlies because that's what their inner impressions, conditioning and beliefs actually are concerning what the spiritual unknown *should* represent.

Personally, I hold the unwavering belief that we're in a totally loving and infinitely supportive cosmos, not a harmful or dangerous one, and all we humans do is use this cosmos to exist.

The infinite Cosmic Intelligence doesn't judge anything to be good or bad, right or wrong the way humans do, it just supports, with absolute neutrality, the materialization of your strongest and most vivid and consistent thought forms. Because it *is* love, the Cosmic Mind doesn't know the lack of love, except through humankind and the lower realms of consciousness. So it automatically assumes that you're self loving enough to be focusing your attention on what you'd love to experience (rather than what you'd not love) and relentlessly goes about empowering you to manifest it. And so, whether it's evil spirits or joyous empowerment, it comes to into being more rapidly and convincingly because of the new and intensified energy you have induced.

MASTER OR VICTIM?

There is no such thing as *bad energy*, there is only energy. Without exception, everything else is judgmental misunderstandings upheld by a human ego. It's that simple.

I realize that this doesn't alter the fact that an entity of negative intent may have manifested, but it's important that the supposed victim should remember that any entity can only be, and is, a product of their own thoughts and beliefs that they'd been harboring, either consciously or unconsciously. It's really only the person challenging themselves with their own fears! That's why "There is nothing to fear but fear itself."

Only fear—aggressive, controlling, judgmental, confrontational, vengeful or angry thoughts, beliefs and attitudes—can cause aggressive, controlling, overpowering, vengeful, stressful, confrontational, and disharmonious experiences.

If you have fearful or disturbing experiences of any kind, just see them as a sign that you still harbor fearful and disturbing thoughts, beliefs and attitudes and they're ready to be eradicated from your consciousness. Accept full responsibility that they have materialized and then accept full responsibility for going about replacing those parts of your consciousness with loving, allowing, abundant, harmonious and compassionate attitudes, thoughts and beliefs; let those be your norm and they will become your life experience.

Any circumstance will become eradicated as soon as the corresponding thought form is eradicated. It's that simple. This spiritual responsibility asks you to realize and personify your own higher consciousness by proving mastery over your entire life according to the Cosmic Law of Creation.

Anyone who complains that they have tried but their unpleasant circumstance doesn't subside is actually defending and energizing their own belief in being a victim, the opposite of a master. They're actually empowering their reality to fill with more experiences where they indeed feel powerless. Victimhood is an ego illusion founded on forgetting and denying the spiritual truth that creation power is the essence of every human being.

Before attempting to move further on their path, such people need to take a long, hard, brutally honest look at their basic beliefs about their spirituality and spiritual responsibilities, their potential and their lives, all the while bearing in mind the Cosmic Law of Creation.

Exposing yourself to higher Light or intensified life force energy can never be harmful. It's absolutely, categorically impossible. It can certainly be disruptive and highlight a person's beliefs about their victimhood and disempowerment being real, instead of their God given creation power being real.

Full blown victimhood is when a person's masculine and feminine energies are both at the low end of the frequency scale; when they're thoroughly in low consciousness.

In terms of their feminine energy, that usually means looking at life as though it's *happening to* them—that they're hopelessly susceptible to the effects of events, people, circumstances, forces, fate, destiny—in fact, of almost anything or everything. They have never got past the misperception that they have no say in their own experiences, and they act accordingly. They often believe they must do whatever they're told by others and that their own time and needs are less important than others'.

Furthermore, in that mindset, a person tends to believe that, because they themselves are a victim of circumstances, everyone else is a victim of circumstances in just the same way! Because that's just *how it is*, right? Wrong. But throughout their life they behave as if it were true anyway. It can manifest as attention seeking; wanting approval; being clingy or needy; feeling that life is unfair. You'll hear it in such sentiments as "They did it to me", "I have to", "It's different for you because you're lucky", "I'm not allowed to", "Why does it always happen to me?", "They made me do it" or "I never get the chance."

Other symptoms include apathy and blame, lack of purpose, and believing others don't understand. Some say "Oh, that poor person", "They need me" or "That shouldn't happen." Obviously, all such attitudes are based on an underlying belief that a person has no power in the circumstance.

In terms of masculine energy, being in victim consciousness means wanting or trying to control others or to control life's circumstances; wanting to know what the future holds; manipulating people or doing things in order to become needed or to achieve some other self-interested outcome; projecting one's self, beliefs, values and attitudes into the world to get attention, validation, approval, authority, security or some other sense of being safe, better or worthwhile. Trying to make someone dependent is a typical insidious example.

All of these attitudes are based on the belief that people are victims of life's circumstances so they'd better make themselves a perpetrator, otherwise they'll become the helpless victim. They feel they must control life to avoid *bad* things happening *to* them and, of course, to try to make sure that *good* things happen *to* them.

Once again judgment—good or bad, right or wrong, better or worse—is the underlying motivational force. And their ego believes it is warranted, even though they're just subjective judgments based on past conditioning or an arbitrary set of rules learned earlier in life. These people refuse to look at this as self limiting patterns of thinking infecting their creation stream because some horribly powerful bullying force is responsible, not they, for these conditions in their life... are they? Because they know what's good and right... so they wouldn't do such bad and wrong things... would they?

This low consciousness problem is compounded by people who, believing they themselves are a victim of circumstances, go on to treat others as though they too are victims. For instance, someone might feel sorry for another in a predicament or might try to fix someone else's problems for them. Parents are often prime examples, treating their children in this way.

How could you ever feel sorry for someone else or believe you need to protect or defend them when you know categorically that only they, and nobody else, can be and has always been the absolute creator of their life through the Cosmic Law of Creation?

You may understand their situation or have a deep compassion for their misunderstanding, but your pity will never help them. It'll only support their ignorance and victimhood and perpetuate their life in helplessness. Instead, use your compassion and understanding of their plight to bring empowerment. Help them see and understand their creation power and relentlessly support them in coming to grips with it throughout their life's circumstances. If not by you, how will they learn that they needn't feel powerless because they're actually the creation force in their own life, able to create anything they choose to focus their attention on?

Another common example is someone believing that they can change another person, or that that they can make things happen *to* or *for* someone else. How could you believe you can *make* (force/control) someone heal or fix their problems unless you also believed that they could be the victim or beneficiary of things happening *to* them?

Only a faulty assumption that the person is powerless in their life would suggest that you can play the part of the outer force that they fear or depend upon for the circumstances happening to them in their life. And that'd be the same assumption that has strengthened their low consciousness belief in being a victim in the first place.

The whole pattern is established in fear; an illusion, a mass falsehood that depends upon everyone believing in victimhood in order for the farce to continue. It's laughable, everyone supporting and encouraging everyone else to believe in exactly what they fear the most—that they're powerless in life. Victims breed victims and support victim status, disempowerment and dependency. Victim consciousness is what drives people to the depths of despair until they feel they can no longer live life for fear of what it might 'dish out to them.'

Mastery is the exact opposite. It's the consciousness of empowerment; being fully aware of the fact that you wield the ultimate power in your life through the Cosmic Law of Creation and that everyone else does too. In its clearest manifestations you'll see a person who knows that they create their own reality by their own self discipline of thoughts, beliefs and attitudes. They know that they have created every single piece of their reality and are responsible for it, and whatever involves another soul is a co-creation. And they behave accordingly.

Masters don't feel sorry for people in predicaments because they know that those people are as powerful and capable as anyone else in creating their own experiences. Therefore they honor that person's choice to create what they have, even if it appears to be a problem, instead of believing there is something wrong with the circumstances.

If someone asks them for help, a true master responds by lovingly reminding or explaining to the person that they're creating the problem themselves and helps them understand how they can begin to create something else by believing in themselves, not some outside force, and disciplining their attitudes and thoughts to enable transformation in an empowering rather than disempowering way.

A master prefers not to fix the problem *for* the person because if they did then, when the person encounters another problem, they'll just feel they're dependent on the master or someone else to fix it for them again next time. That's not freedom and it certainly is not being independent nor in one's power. It's dependency and being powerless to do anything about the circumstances without the assistance of some outside power again. In the words of British statesman & author, Benjamin Disraeli, *"The greatest good you can do for another is not just to share your riches, but to reveal to him his own."*

Mastery in feminine energy is being aware of and open to feelings, people and circumstances without compromising your higher understanding or your sense of love and empowerment. It also means, in all circumstances, being open to all possible answers, truths or solutions, even irrational or differing ones, without feeling in need, in conflict or compromised by them. It means being open to change and to the potential of the universe to deliver miraculous things as and when it's appropriate for one and all. It means taking responsibility for all your own creations and being wholly honest with yourself about the likely effects of all actions taken. In a nutshell, staying attuned to and acting on the guidance and impulses of your inner authority, your Higher Self, rather than those of your ego.

Mastery in masculine energy means constantly disciplining yourself to focus on thoughts of inner truth, self power, compassion and love, and creating your reality regardless of what outside influences or circumstances seem to dictate. The masculine energy principle in mastery is not the dictator of what's right or wrong, good or bad, it's the force that acts with courage and commitment upon the higher wisdom and insights made available by the open, receptive feminine energy. It means doing so whilst treating others with the compassion and respect they deserve as the equal master they are, whether they know it or not.

The responsible masculine energy in mastery doesn't become overbearing or inflexible, it simply brings things to reality through self discipline, focus, structure, communication and action; actualizing self power through the way you're being in your life. It enacts higher consciousness in the world. It is power in, not power over.

A common scenario is in the area of healing. A healer may feel sorry for a patient with a condition, or feel that it's their job or responsibility to fix the problem. This is fear and victim consciousness.

Firstly, they're believing that life happens *to* people and therefore needs to be avoided or controlled and, secondly, that they can fix it on behalf of the sufferer (that is, that they can 'do the fixing *to* them'). Their most highly conscious action is to observe the person in that condition and, without passing judgment and without the biases of their own emotional energy infecting their actions, treat the person as though they have manifested the condition themselves and are fully able to correct it themselves or manifest an alternative. The healer then is simply standing in for the patient at a time when the patient has forgotten their own power of mastery or requests additional energy with which to work on the condition they have manifested.

Nobody can heal anybody else because that means doing something *to* someone, which is victim consciousness and would conflict with the unalterable gift of free will. Though they might like to think they have, a healer has neither the capability nor the responsibility to heal anyone; they can however provide the service of opportunity and energy which a person's Higher Self will draw upon and use in ways that are perfect for their highest good at the time.

Unfortunately, victim consciousness is woven thoroughly throughout our world. Take insurance for example. An insurer relies on clientele believing that life will be a *bad* experience, not a good one; that it will do things to people or to their possessions. This not only illustrates but also depends upon people's beliefs being negative, fearful and disempowered. In insidious ways, it supports and encourages low consciousness and a sense of helplessness in the population. When you pay for any insurance policy, you're actually gambling; you're betting the insurance company that you'll have something go wrong. Yet the company is betting you it won't! Insurers do not take risks unless the odds are seriously in their favor. That being the case, though they promote fear because it's good for business, the insurance company actually has more faith in a positive outcome in a person's life than the person buying the insurance has!

Ultimately, the only real insurance you'll ever have is your ability and discipline to deliberately create every single circumstance and experience in your life through your own positive and uplifting thoughts and actions. Only with that knowledge, with healthy courage and unfailing faith in the Cosmic Law of Creation can you be sure of a life of fulfillment, joy, love and abundance without serious deviations or upsets. *"The more you depend on forces outside of yourself, the more you are dominated by them,"* observed Harold Sherman.

At least let yourself realize that you are *allowed* to move out of misery and victimhood and into a state of self realized mastery, even if you're not yet ready to embrace such freedom or its associated readjustments in your life. Just by allowing it to be a possibility, you'll gradually allow the new consciousness to filter gently in and displace the old.

If you persist, then bit by bit you'll gain command of your life and begin to feel the sense of liberation that it brings.

People expect the new energies and potential of the new age of Light to dispel their fears and negativities *for* them. But it can not and will not. It will just supercharge whatever you're choosing to be—a person willing to change by transmuting negative beliefs into positive ones, or a person not yet willing to release their beliefs that life is happening to them in a series of unpredictable events that need to be controlled or avoided.

In either instance, your power to manifest is increased by the influx of new light, and it's your responsibility to be aware of it and to wield it with love, compassion and wisdom, not with control, fear or ignorance.

When the higher vibrations of Light become available to you, *you* are the one responsible for having chosen to induce that Light; *you* are the one responsible for maintaining loving and supportive beliefs regarding yourself, life and the nature of the energy and its source. *You* are the one responsible for finding out about and deciding how you'll handle the effects of the energy and *you* are the one responsible for how it manifests throughout your life. *You* are the one responsible for your self discipline, courage, focus and will to make a difference. *You* are the one responsible for your *Self Watching*, *Mind Shifting* and *Honest Actions*.

The truth is that you actually always have been

responsible; the difference now may be that you've become aware of it.

The energy and its Source will never decide what it will represent in your life; that would be to overrule your free will. Instead, it simply fuels who you're *choosing* to be so that you can become more of it; what you're *choosing* to focus on so that you can have more of it.

You are responsible for finding and being the type of self that can become a fulfilled master of your reality or the type that'll fight for their fears, difficulties and limitations and remain a victim. You are responsible for your own choices. If you choose the latter, how will you justify complaining about a life of misery or struggle, dullness or disappointment?

You are the only one who can determine what you believe and think about. It's all very well to argue that others convince you, force, coerce or trick you into thinking or believing something. It's fine to suggest that you have all the conditioning of past and present life experiences that determine your responses and beliefs.

But that's just victim consciousness rearing its ugly disempowering head again in the name of blame—a victim's view of responsibility. Whether the influence is a person or doctrine, part of our physical realm, part of another realm of consciousness or of some cultural belief system, ultimately *you* still decide what *you* will accept or refute, think or believe.

Many say that they're presently the result of

all the influences that have gone before, and that's true. However, to take a more responsible look at that premise, we're all actually the result of all the influences we've *chosen* to believe in and adhere to up to the present moment.

Everyone is responsible for choosing what beliefs they'll maintain and which they'll change; that's exercising free will. Furthermore, the understanding, light technology and healing modalities are now available to grow through those disempowering victim beliefs and into ones of self mastery.

It's *your* responsibility to choose and find ways to get out of the mass victimhood and powerlessness mindset rather than to hide in the perverse comfort and solace that so many find within it. Nobody and nothing can do it for you because if they did they'd be overruling your gift of free will—something even God won't do. You'd immediately give your power to them by needing them to do it for you the next time you felt powerless in some way.

If you want to have power throughout your life instead of feeling helpless in any situation, then whenever you think you're being attacked or victimized, remember and accept that it's the result of your own past beliefs and attitudes and ask yourself "Why have I created this? What belief or attitude am I learning to let go of or modify *in myself* so that this won't happen again?"

There is nothing in the cosmos that can harm you or has control or authority over you... unless you believe there is and choose to accept it in that light.

Ultimately, it's each individual who is responsible for their own life-full of experiences.

If you choose to open to life, in what way do you choose to respond to the induction of the new consciousness and the intensified energy it introduces? Is it with absolute unbridled wonder, spontaneity, allowance and fresh innocence that says you're an unlimited free spirit of the cosmos? Or with your conditioning that may be telling you that you can't or you're not allowed; that you're not good enough or not the right one; that you don't know enough nor have enough experience; that it will rock the boat too much or endanger you in some way?

Do you want to be a victim or a master? If you want to master your fears and your life and overcome limitations then start acting like it, regardless of outer circumstances or influences. It's *your* choice, *your* responsibility.

Every moment is your choice or the result of your previous choices. And you don't have to perpetuate or hold on to it; you can change your mind again at any moment you choose in favor of a completely different set of beliefs and thoughts. *You* are the boss of your consciousness in all its myriad facets. It's also okay if you choose to be ensconced in the old mass mentality of victimhood—it's easier! But you can never complain about your life circumstances without abusing, hurting and lying to yourself. That's spiritual responsibility.

Opening to life requires you be the master; discipline your own thoughts and attitudes in life rather than letting your thoughts and attitudes be determined by your outer world of influences. After all, by the Cosmic Law of Creation, and the cosmic principle of 'as above, so below,' the outer world follows you naturally; it doesn't lead you unless you let it. By the Law of cause and effect, your outer world is the effect and your inner world is the cause.

Thought precedes experience, and as you move more thoroughly into the higher frequencies of consciousness those thoughts will become materialized more rapidly and vividly than ever before as your experience. The increased intensities of life force energy you'll be channeling and working with will ensure that.

"God helps those who help themselves" means that the Supreme Intelligence will unfailingly bring in everything possible to support those who accept, take responsibility for and use the immutable spiritual Laws and forces that govern all existence, understanding that they create every iota of their reality.

Keep making moves in the direction your heart urges and the cosmos will keep bringing to you all manner of support. It relates to you only through your images and heart so if your direction is not established from heart in imaginable picture form, then the cosmos will not support you. You can't turn your back on your innate Supreme power unless you resort to self denial and the lower fear consciousness and victimhood that are its servants and the seeds of all ills.

I recall one woman who had a terminal disease.

Consistently, healthcare professionals advised her that, in order to turn her health around, she needed to stop eating a few simple things that her body could not digest and were poisonous to her. She insisted she was *unable* to stop eating them for cultural reasons.

'Unable' was her victim translation for *choosing* not to discipline herself to stop eating these things, no matter the consequences. Yet she continually blamed the disease for her unhappiness and pain; always wanted help and healing for her illness, and people to pity her being in such a predicament.

This too was taking responsibility—for her own demise. Surely she could not justify blaming the disease when she had such an obvious key to her own problem! All she needed was the will to harness the new knowledge and to discipline herself to rearrange her eating habits. But the dietary approach to her disease, along with the spiritual responsibility for it, were very new ideas to her.

She was obviously not ready yet to allow them to displace the old comfortable beliefs about her victimhood and limitedness, and that her woes could and should be corrected by some outside authority or external force. Such clear guidance is rare in anyone's life, but she was not ready nor flexible enough to embrace it, even though it would've answered her plight so directly and completely. She died.

After all the channel openings I've facilitated in many different countries around the world, I've come to know beyond a shadow of doubt that the benefits of the energy are determined by each individual's courage and discipline to stay connected and clear. Then, taking the same courage and discipline, actualize the new consciousness through their own everyday experiences instead of becoming discouraged by the conditioned, habitual fears and limitations of the old ways of believing. Nobody but the individual can be responsible for that self assertion.

Should you choose to *live* the path of Light (rather than just think or talk about it), you'll find it one of ever increasing fulfillment through transformation, spontaneity and allowance; a path that requires your acceptance of your role as the force that determines every experience in your life and your service of reminding others that theirs is fundamentally the same.

When you are given the required materials and tools, only you can choose to use them and only you can decide how diligently. You are responsible for identifying and releasing the parts of your consciousness that hold you back from your own emergence into Light and your full embracement of the love, abundance, peace, wellbeing and mastery that can only come through opening to channel New Light, new life.

> *"Wholeheartedly invoke, embrace and evoke*
> *the new vibrations of Light and you will reclaim*
> *absolute sovereignty over every moment of your*
> *reality in this lifetime."*

~ The Master Merlin

NOW & BEYOND

Channeling is neither mysterious nor unnatural. Nor is it reserved for only a few special or select people. It has attracted attention in recent years as more and more individuals have found themselves in communication with higher realms of consciousness. These spheres of intelligence have become more present among humankind with the intention of assisting us through our present phase of evolution, a shift in consciousness that promises a love based world instead of the fear based one to which we've become accustomed.

The most obvious manifestation of their presence in our midst seems to have been the verbal channeling that continues to become increasingly prevalent as this shift progresses. As our vibrations rise, so we come closer in resonance to theirs and we become able to interface more effectively with them to access their vast knowingness and expand our relatively puny version. They utilize every opportunity to convey alternative perspectives on life and our self image, channeling their unfamiliar wisdom into our minds to be translated by us into words and phrases that are more familiar in order to help us become more aware and grow in context with the Supreme Plan of Light of which we're all a vital part.

Channeling is not just words, however. Most people think that's what it is because it's the popularized form. But words are only a small part of the function of channeling.

Channeling, in the context of the new rising

consciousness and energy in our world, would be more accurately described as allowing in higher forms of the life force energy in service to the spiritual evolution of self, humankind and the Earth. Even in direct voice channeling, the popularized form where a human channel vocally transmits information or guidance from another intelligence in higher realms of consciousness, the words are still just floating on the energy like leaves upon a flowing stream. Just as the stream is the underlying force, not the leaves, so it's the energy transmitted that's most significant in the channeling process, not the words themselves.

The channeled words, though quite likely being useful guidance, mainly serve to fascinate and distract the thinking minds of the listeners while the energy goes about doing the real work of raising the vibration of everyone's consciousness.

The energy is undoubtedly the most significant part of the transmission. It acts like a blending agent for the words to be absorbed into the consciousness of each individual in whatever way is most healing and meaningful to them. This remarkable transmission of energy in the new age phenomenon of channeling or interdimensional telepathy gives it an immeasurable and uncontrollable healing benefit on all kinds of inner levels that the human mind would never even consider.

Being a frequent channel for these beings myself, it never ceases to amaze and impress me since it has never been something I've set out to do, nor is it something that my present framework of believing allows me think I could yet achieve myself, even if I did intend to. I just surrender to it and trust its effectiveness.

The effects of a channeling session, particularly an individual private one, on a person's life or even on the circumstances surrounding a place, time or situation are also remarkable. Amazing transformations of a totally unpredictable and unexpected nature take place as the most extraordinary conditions—ones that could never have been planned or manipulated into place, or even dreamed of—develop over a period of months, weeks, days or even moments.

One man in Australia, hankering for progress in his life after two years unemployed and unhappy, attended one of my Cosmic Activation workshops in his area. Following the workshop, he diligently used the simple exercises he'd learned and only a few days later, the kind of job he'd wanted mysteriously landed in his life. He'd dissolved whatever unseen block had been standing between himself and that particular area of fulfillment.

In another instance, a woman in India came to my Cosmic Activation workshop and carried on the simple daily procedure in which the workshop culminates. Within two weeks she'd repaired a longstanding serious heart disease. This undoubtedly came about by her allowing changes to take place in her way of being, thereby dissolving blocks that had been holding that aspect of her consciousness in a diseased state.

Miracles? No. Just energy guided by discipline, diligence and spiritual responsibility. It's not my doing at all but their own *Self Watching, Mind Shifting* and *Honest Actions* brought to bear in their daily lives, energized by their opening to channel pure life force energy.

That illustrates the magic that a person can consciously create in their own life if they're prepared to *allow* change to happen rather than trying to *make* it happen. Allowing it to happen requires the person channeling the energy into their daily life, all the while putting aside from the channeling process any judgments, apprehensions, biases, needs or fears they have had and letting life flow in unbridled spontaneity.

In both cases I described, it took their own choosing to attend the workshop and their own choosing to diligently apply what they learned to the day-to-day experiences that make up their life.

That takes self love and self nurturing plus a deep desire and courage to change their causality—their old mindset and behavior. It also requires self discipline to transcend, in everyday situations, the ego's will to uphold the old ways of the victimhood status quo. Strength is needed to overcome the ego's resistance to changing itself because it believes it's powerless and its outer world should change to support it.

Achieving such remarkable transformation in their lives also required that they took responsibility for bringing through the highest levels of Light and consciousness (life force energy) of which they're capable, rather than the levels that they'd been comfortable with, the ones they themselves could understand or the ones they thought would best suit the circumstances and not rock the boat.

I believe that there is nothing dangerous in the cosmos. I never expect to magnetize negative or bad experiences to myself. Nor do I ever regard any of my experiences as being bad or negative, though they might be exceedingly uncomfortable or disruptive at times. I'm nothing specially different or gifted, just diligent and disciplined where it matters to me.

If you harbor fears of danger then you'll create experiences that'll appear dangerous to you. In times of extensive change or of great upheaval or turmoil in life, many people ask for protection from harm. They need to be very aware though not to actually base it on the thought of protection from anything that's *uncomfortable* or *disruptive*. In the instances of the man manifesting his job and the woman healing her disease, both individuals experienced disruption and discomfort in their lives as the changes were taking place.

Without actually disrupting things as they are, nothing will change; without letting go of the consciousness of unemployment, a job can't manifest; without letting go of disease, healing can't take place. Just as an adverse situation is not necessarily negative or bad, neither do the disruptive effects of change in life need to be harmful or negative. It's impossible to attract negative experiences without having the seed of that negativity in you already, so start right now taking responsibility for your life.

Take stock of your own belief systems, thought habits and conditioning. Claim responsibility for them then willingly claim responsibility for altering the ones that do not support the qualities of life that a joyous and fulfilled you would be experiencing.

Beginning immediately, eradicate all negative, evil, dangerous, disallowing, conflicting and fearful thoughts from your mind concerning absolutely everything, no exceptions, no compromises. You'll automatically begin to eradicate experiences of those same qualities from your own life.

If it weren't so sad it might be humorous that those involved in spiritual activities and occupations expect some supposed outside force to do something for them, defend them or rescue them from unwanted experiences when in truth (and ironically, in their particular case of supposed spiritual awareness) it's their own Supreme Power and free will that enables all their experiences to manifest in the first place; no exceptions!

Just as it is with everyone else, the thought forms and beliefs these people harbor bring all things to them. Nobody but they can apply or change their minds and that's the basis of their free will. If they keep allowing their thinking to wander onto negative entities or dangerous energies or whatever else their minds can dream up, then nothing in the cosmos is going to undermine their right to focus on and believe in those things and thereby magnetize the experience of them.

They can also dissolve that danger just as easily when they're prepared to stop playing victim to other consciousness and the process of spiritual emergence. When they're prepared to cease subordinating themselves to some ideology or outer power; when they're willing to give up the need or desire to make spiritual enlightenment look special or mysterious or important; when they're ready to acknowledge the ultimate power—the master within—and live it... the fears will disappear once and for all.

All elements of our universe are organized to support our free will and the power of personal creation through the process of life. Nothing is static or the same as it was; not our potential, our needs, capabilities, understandings, values, even our societies or nations. Time itself is not as it was. When we realize this, we can either harness the force of perpetual change and together steer it to the benefit of one and all or we can abuse it to our mutual detriment. Once again, it's up to our own free will.

While the ambient energies of our consciousness and our world are rising and intensifying, time itself is accelerating. As a result, we can accomplish much more in a given time frame than we could previously. All it takes is for us all to work mutually with the power of intention and to work with life on an energy level where the stuff that life is made of is much more malleable and responsive to intention.

When you know without a shadow of doubt that it's you who creates your reality by focusing your attention, then plain common sense will guide you to focus your attention on more fulfilling things and disappointment, conflict and negativity will distract you less. Plus, when you believe in your heart beyond any shadow of doubt that the energy is intensifying, you'll develop enormous faith in it materializing in your life. You'll also become increasingly aware of your *intentional* manifestations instead of treating them as coincidences.

The greatest liberation in this process is the realization that you personally will undergo enormous and rapid transformation if you choose to adhere to the cosmic principles, despite any surrounding influences to the contrary.

Times are changing—accelerating. No longer do you need to spend ages in ceremony, ritual or practice to open your own channels to new frequencies of Light and bring healing and new potentiality to your life.

It can happen instantaneously. Instantaneously! I've seen it myself, more times than I care to recall. You are still required to go through the disciplines and procedures that open the cosmic doors of spiritual initiation and personal transformation, because a key must still be inserted in the lock and turned if the door is to open.

But now the door can be unlocked much more quickly, and anyone can turn the key as soon as they know it and are willing. You can do it. All you need do is choose to do it, choose to believe that it will be quick and effortless, and go ahead.

Unfortunately, many people on their spiritual crusade try to hold newcomers back by saying "Oh, that step will take blah blah blah years, then this step another blah blah more..." and so on. That's rubbish. It's old-energy thinking spilling over from the burgeoning dust heaps of the old paradigm.

Their reason for such warnings or disciplines is their own misunderstandings based upon it having taken them that long to achieve the result themselves, or that someone else or some obsolete doctrine told them that same thing and they chose to believe it. In many instances they're simply being controlling of the new energy. This attitude can be found in people now awakening to their spirituality but still resistant to its full power and potential to establish a foundation of personal, independent, self enabled limitlessness.

I've personally witnessed numerous instances of astonishing spiritual awakenings and self realizations happen literally overnight in regular people who never thought of themselves as anything unusual or spiritual. All over the world this is taking place. I'm not the only one who sees these miracles, I'm sure, so it must be happening almost *en mass* nowadays.

Ordinary people are having extraordinary awakenings, just by changing their minds about themselves; by embracing their reality and potential to shine as a brilliant jewel in the crown of a new consciousness, an inspired and heightened existence on our planet.

Remember constantly to think only well of yourself and your life and your potential in all circumstances and to dream only dreams of effortless, speedy, joyous fulfillment in every impossible way. Then it will become so.

Think only well of others and hold the intention that all your actions and behavior be based on well meaning and unconditionally loving compassion and understanding, on harmony and mutual empowerment for one and all, and on the eradication of the spiritual ignorance and impotence that continues to plague humankind the world over. Then it will become so.

In all circumstances, act with self love and unfailing integrity, never suppressing your Inner Truth but always being flexible enough to deliver it with courage and integrity—never with compromise or the intention to inflict or conflict; always with compassion and the intention that it be loving and healing. Then it will become so.

Constantly hold the thought and vision of your own physical body and subtle energy field glowing with love and wisdom and potency, and the cells of your body radiating a light of Love and perfect form and function, and that these get stronger and stronger with every breath you take. Then it will become so.

Think of brilliant light in every cell of your body eradicating all past conditioning and dissolving all disease. Then it will become so.

Train yourself to listen only to your inner impulse in every instant. If an outside influence doesn't resonate with your deepest inner approval, then do not entertain it as true and appropriate for you. Let it be. Realize that it might be the truth that someone else requires for their next step or that it may mean something to you at another time. You will see it become so.

Remember that every time you act on your Inner Truth and impulses instead of outer influences, it enables everyone around you to become more free of the fear, pain, struggle and untruths that have plagued their past. As they move past that conditioning, they too can begin to radiate their own vital light more purely and brightly. Imagine your own Inner Voice becomes louder and clearer as a result. Then it will become so.

Hold the thoughts and images of a fountain of Light pouring out of the top of your head and flowing over and through your body, uninhibited by material form, and on into the Earth's heart to bring her healing. Imagine a stream of pure Light, as you take every breath, pouring in through the top of your head and supercharging your entire energy system and all the cells of your body with new consciousness, love and healing. Then it will become so.

In every moment of every day, see yourself as a radiant, translucent, physical being on the planet, not a dense physical one. When you see or hear of unhappy or traumatic events in people's lives or around the world, don't feel sorry for them or angry, upset or disappointed, frustrated or worried. Those feelings have never helped anyone in constructive ways. Instead, see your Inner Light and radiance intensifying and growing so that it floods those circumstances with Divine healing and love and peace. Then it will become so.

Use such thought forms, mental practices and disciplines in every moment of every day. If you find yourself becoming disheartened or disillusioned, down or sorrowful, then fill your mind again with the images and thoughts of what you have that *is* positive, what you experience that you *do* appreciate or love, even if it's as simple as having a friend to talk to, a meal on the table, a roof over your head or a clear blue sky. The universe will then see your thought forms and bring you more and more about which you'll feel positive and appreciative.

The time has come for one and all to truly open to life in all its unpredictable glory, and be at peace with all that transpires. Life is life, and the least that'll happen as a result of this most spiritual of activities will be a little more life. But Infinite Life is the real aim.

The practices I've outlined cost nothing but openness, fresh thinking, flexibility and a little time, trust, courage and discipline. Choose to use them whenever you're doubtful, fearful, angry, critical or sad in regard to yourself or others; add the principles of Higher Light and the thought forms of higher consciousness and a new unlimited ocean of possibilities will begin to manifest in your life... more often, more vividly and more quickly.

And be sure to acknowledge when they do because when you're aware of them beginning to materialize and you acknowledge it consciously, you're reclaiming *conscious* power, becoming a deliberate walker in Light and your own energy will radiate like a beacon. Your personal energy will begin to influence those around you positively and effortlessly just by being the Light, and by opening to life in all its natural, effortless glory.

*Only when you are totally at peace
with all of Life without wishing to harness,
control, rationalize or define the uncertainty
of its infinite nature, shall you truly
be powerful and free.*

EXPERIENTIAL WORKSHOPS

Paul Walsh-Roberts presents workshops, seminars and services around the world which actualize the principles covered in this book throughout people's daily lives. The range of workshops includes:

COSMIC ACTIVATION
Opening Your Channels To Higher Guidance & Transformation

This is the workshop that this book is all about, bringing its essential principles into your real experience. Get in touch with your own Inner Guidance and the Masters in Light who are in service to humanity at these crucial times. Experience the tangible physical effects of high frequency energy and learn how to use and direct it at will for guidance, vitality and inspiration, and for healing and vocal/written channelling.

LIGHTBODY HEALING
Self Healing On All Levels

Use your subtle energy bodies to transmute your own physical, emotional and mental healing issues with speed and ease. Be in service to the whole of humanity, as well as Mother Earth. Learn a powerful, rapid and effective way of transmuting the effects of the Human Ascension in your own daily life.

If you'd like information about either Paul or his wife Alexandria, their other books and CDs, and the array of life enrichment and spiritual empowerment workshops, seminars and consultations each conducts around the world, please visit:

www.lifeoflight.com

There, you'll also find how you can participate directly in the global healing and consciousness shift. If you'd like to know Paul & Alexandria's schedule of activities and events around the world, or bring their work to your area, then e-mail directly:

info@lifeoflight.com

Printed in the United Kingdom
by Lightning Source UK Ltd.
111052UKS00001B/4-57